LEAVING BEHIND A RIGHTEOUS LEGACY

"Each of us leaves some landmarks or legacies wherever we go, whether we know it or not, and whether we like it or not."

ARMSTRONG CHEGGEH

Published by
Olivia Kimbrell Press™

Olivia Kimbrell Press™

COPYRIGHT NOTICE

Leaving Behind a Righteous Legacy

First edition. Copyright © 2016 by Armstrong Cheggeh. All rights reserved. No part of this publication may be reproduced or transmitted in any form or by any means — electronic, mechanical, photocopying, or recording — without express written permission of the author. The only exception is brief quotations in printed or broadcasted critical articles and reviews. This book is a work of nonfiction. Specific names and places of individuals and towns may have been changed in order to protect the privacy of those involved or where required by law in the case of minor children.

PUBLISHED BY: Olivia Kimbrell Press™*, P.O. Box 470, Fort Knox, KY 40392-0470

The Olivia Kimbrell Press™ colophon and open book logo are trademarks of Olivia Kimbrell Press™.

Olivia Kimbrell Press™ is a publisher offering true to life, meaningful fiction and non-fiction from a Christian worldview intended to uplift the heart and engage the mind.

Library Cataloging Data

Names: Cheggeh, Armstrong (Armstrong Cheggeh) 1956-

Title: Leaving Behind a Righteous Legacy / Armstrong Cheggeh

Description: Olivia Kimbrell Press digital eBook edition | Olivia Kimbrell Press Trade paperback edition | Kentucky: Olivia Kimbrell Press, 2016.

Summary: What we say, do, and even think in life remains after we depart.

Identifiers: LCCN 2016938574 | ISBN-13: 978-1-68190-031-5 (trade) | 978-1-68190-032-2 (POD) | 978-1-68190-033-9 (ebk.)

Subjects: LCSH: Theology, Doctrinal sh85134686 Christian doctrines; Christianity–Doctrines; Doctrinal theology; Doctrines, Christian; Dogmatic theology; Fundamental theology; Systematic theology; Theology, Dogmatic; Theology, Systematic | Word of God (Christian theology) sh85148103 God's Word (Christian theology); Word of God (Theology); Word of the Lord (Christian theology) BISAC: REL012040 RELIGION / Christian Life / Inspirational | REL012120 RELIGION / Christian Life / Spiritual Growth | REL012120 RELIGION / Christian Life / Spiritual Growth | REL070000 RELIGION / Christianity / General | BIC: HRAB1 | HRCG9 | HRCL | HRCS | HRCV | HRCV9 | HRCX6 | HRLD | THEMA: QRAM | QRMP | QRVG | QRVS2 | QRVS3 | QRVX | QRVJ | QRVK

Classification: LCC Z688.C53 B72 2015 | 248.8'43—dc211

LEAVING BEHIND A RIGHTEOUS LEGACY

ARMSTRONG CHEGGEH

I speak God's favor and blessing over your life!

Bishop A.K. Cheggeh
I Cor 10:31

Armstrong Cheggeh

Endorsements

I can think of no one better qualified to speak about legacy and the perpetual power of a godly life than Bishop Armstrong Cheggeh.

Having watched his life and ministry explode over the last 30 years, I can emphatically say that the mantle of spiritual fatherhood on his life is a hallmark reason for his great success as an apostle and leader of men. Because he and his virtuous wife, Mama Rhoda, have exemplified the principles set forth in this book, their legacy will live on through the hundreds of spiritual sons and daughters they have nurtured through the years. The Word of God promises that the righteous will be "in everlasting remembrance" (Psalm 112:6), a promise predicated, in part, to a life well lived and wholly committed to the Lord.

Such a life passes down a kind of spiritual DNA to its descendants, guaranteeing the perpetuation of its blessing, strength and anointing in coming generations. Bishop Cheggeh's timely book will both enlighten and enable all of us, man and woman alike, to reach for greater effectiveness at leaving a godly and goodly legacy to those coming up behind us. Read it and rise to the challenge.

—DR. MALCOLM W. HILL
PASTOR, WORD OF FAITH CHURCH & REVIVAL CENTER
MONTEREY, VA.

Insightful, Encouraging, Timely, Inspiring. These are just a few words that I use to describe Bishop Cheggeh's latest book, "Leaving Behind a Righteous Legacy." I have always been encouraged by the insight and wisdom of Bishop Cheggeh and this book will only add to my respect and admiration of my dear friend. He joins experience from both African and American culture to bring to us the challenge of leaving behind a legacy that will last for generations and bring glory to God.

—REV. LARRY HASEMEYER
SENIOR PASTOR, GATEWAY FELLOWSHIP
MILLERSBURG, OHIO

The great value of Dr. Cheggeh's latest book is its look into the biblical basis of a godly heritage. There is a needful word here for the present generation which will enlarge our vision for the future. This book is must-read for every Christian leader who desires to leave a righteous legacy.

—REV. CLARK IVEY
PRESIDENT, COMPASSION WORLD OUTREACH

No one learns without example, for reference acts as guide and enhances the urge to launch in the unfamiliar, the unknown and new areas. This book will greatly assist those who care to follow and leave behind models that are worth emulating. It is inspirational and awakens the desire to leave a mark that adds value to the society as a whole.

—REV. PETER MBEDE
DIRECTOR FOR THE YOUTH
FOUNTAIN OF LIFE CHURCHES INT'L, NAIROBI

In this magnificent, theological and biblical artifact, Bishop Dr. Armstrong has finally made a case of multidisciplinary analysis of biblical exegesis both in and outside the church. By using Joshua/Caleb story, he makes a compelling case for leadership legacy and challenges the church's status quo in caring for the "least of these".

—DR. JOSEPH NZEKETHA
MIRACLE CENTER, WORLD COMPASSION OUTREACH
MINISTRIES, PLAINFIELD, NJ

There is a cliché that says common sense is not common. One of the more common reactions to getting the answer to a riddle or the secret behind a magicians' trick is, "of course, I could have told you that." Yet we did not give the answer or know the trick. It is easy to miss the mark without a map; this book is such a map. In this book are words of wisdom that if taken to heart will be a map one can use to lay a good foundation now and into the future.

Bishop Armstrong Kamau Cheggeh wears many hats ranging from the leader of a large ministry to an author and teacher but to me he is simply Dad. That title, as I am finding out, comes with the greatest responsibility of all the titles we can hold and in regards to legacy it is supreme. A father has tremendous influence on his children for good or ill. I therefore do not endorse this book simply for its content; I endorse this book because of the character of the man. I am what I am today in great part to what my father invested into me; my family, my coworkers, my neighbors are daily affected by the seeds planted by my father.

My father has physically lifted a metal gate that fell on me; he has driven hundreds of miles to bring me what I have needed; I have been able to call at any time to talk; he has been married to the same woman for over thirty-four years and raised children that are now engaged members of society. And maybe most importantly he has provided the environment that has allowed us to grow into the individuals God has led us to become.

We do not always get to say thank you to those that have come before but I can say "Thank you Dad, for investing a godly legacy in us that we will, by God's grace pass down to the next generation." We all pass away; what lasts is what is invested in the lives of those around us; Dad has left such an enduring righteous legacy.

Finally, there is an African proverb that says, "Those who respect the elderly pave their own road toward success." Listen to the words in this book and pave your own road to success.

—COLLINS KAMAU (Son to the Author)
PROJECT MANAGER
POMEROY/COMMONWEALTH OFFICE OF TECHNOLOGY,
FRANKFORT, KY

This book encompasses an extemporary reflection of both the life and ministry of Rev Rhoda and Dr. Armstrong Cheggeh. By examining the fruits of their labor, you quickly discover the selfless legacy imprinted on transformed lives across the Globe. From dinning with very poor in the ghettos of Africa to dinning with world leaders, Bishop Armstrong Cheggeh has remained a transformative influence with tangible evidence for all those who come behind him.

—DR. JACK KARIUKI EDWARDS
PSYCHORERAPIST, LAKE ACWORTH BEHAVIORAL HEALTH SERVICE
ACWORTH, GA

"A good *man* leaves an inheritance to his children's children." (Proverbs 13:22) That inheritance, as Bishop Armstrong describes in the figure of Caleb, "was much bigger than himself and would also outlive him." Greater than the inheritance we leave *for* our children is the one we should leave *in* them. That eternal legacy has been identified so aptly for us in this book as God on our side and Jesus, a faithful friend.

–REV. DR. SOLOMON WAIGWA
RHEMA GOSPEL CHURCH
PONDER, TX.

Everyone will leave something behind in this world when their time is over either good or bad. On the other hand, there are those who will leave behind "a gift of righteous legacy" that will create an impact far greater than the accomplishments of the person who lived it and passed it on.

Dr. Armstrong Cheggeh is a gift to the Body of Christ and God's anointed Ambassador to this world. He is also living out a life that is truly a righteous legacy. He has a remarkable heart to give of himself beyond the call of duty and is paving a way for so many as he demonstrates true leadership that is righteous, courageous and prosperous. This is the kind of man who any leader should follow!

This is a must read book for leaders who are looking beyond their present success. It highlights the essential building blocks to use in one's life to become more than a monument, but a movement of God that transcends from generation to generations. This book will make any great leader a "smarter" leader, because a smart leader can take who he is and all he has done and multiply it exponentially!

I'm glad that Bishop Armstrong has written this book, we all need to hear what he has to say about the idea of leaving behind a righteous legacy!

—DR. DAN SANDOVAL
FOUNDER & PRESIDENT, TAPESTRY FOUNDATION & BUSINESS OWNER
TAPESTRY INT'L

It is a great honor to endorse a book for a person of Bishop Dr. Cheggeh's caliber. I can attest to ethos of this book because I have closely associated with Dr. Cheggeh for more than forty years.

One of the most significant aspects that demonstrate Dr. Cheggeh's credibility in pursuit of leaving a righteous or godly legacy is the manner in which he and his wife have raised their children. All their children have honored the God of their parents and as a matter of fact all of them are serving the Lord in their own ways. Bishop Cheggeh and his wife Rhoda can associate with John who has stated in his epistle, that he found it great joy that his children were walking in truth.

As a person committed to Judeo Christian orthodoxy, Dr. Cheggeh recognizes the centrality of the Holy Scriptures as the principle guide of our faith and practice. Any time I visit his family in Nicholasville, Kentucky, dinning together, a set time for family altar is consistent every day. Dr. Cheggeh is an outstanding leader and all those who work under him enjoy his confidence. He never shies away from confronting issues that may come up that are inconsistent to the true faith, doctrine, and the proper way of doing ministry.

As my mentor and close confidant, my journey of friendship with Dr. Cheggeh has evidenced sincerity and selflessness. His boldness gives those he oversees, the courage to exercise ministry without fear and anxiety. This book is an expression of the personality of my good friend, Dr. Cheggeh and an authentic representation of what he believes and stands for. I thank God for my good friend, and wish him God's favor as he continues to equip leaders through his books. It is my sincere hope that that this book will get into the shelves of many libraries and book stores, so that many people can easily access it. Leaving Behind a Righteous Legacy is must read for every pastor or Christian leader.

—REV. DR. GEOFFREY KAMAU NJUGUNA
DELIVERANCE CHURCH, LANGATA

Dr. Armstrong Cheggeh's book, *"Leaving Behind a Righteous Legacy"* addresses a vital subject whose underlying principle began long time ago, even during the times of Moses – an underlying principle whose distinctive thread can be found interwoven throughout the Biblical story. Throughout the scriptures, there is a recurring emphasis on laying the right foundations on which successive generations can build on. Since inclinations to act in a right away in life only follows from rightly perceiving our life's circumstances in relation to correct understandings of Biblical principles, Dr. Cheggeh has delineated these relevant Bible principles in a way that inculcates an understanding that lead believers to take positive action to bequeath to their future generations a befitting righteous legacy—the right relationship with God, prosperity and God's blessings.

As Joshua and Caleb refused to succumb to doubts and unbelief but focused their faith on God's word and promises, Dr. Cheggeh challenges us to stand for truth, even in the face of opposition. The book achieves its goal of encouraging believers to become better stewards of what God entrusted to them, and to ensure that they bequeath to their families a legacy of righteousness and faithfulness.

The book challenges believers to emulate various Biblical

examples, such as that of Caleb, whose legendary patience, sacrifice and faith allowed him to possess his inheritance, even after forty-five years of patience contemplation. Ultimately, God demonstrated his willingness to keep his promises as he will do for us. To leave an enduring legacy, saints of God must demonstrate unselfish commitment, self-sacrifice for others, patience and faithfulness in serving God. In pursuit of God's will and purpose, Dr. Cheggeh asserts that believers must not give up hope or be discouraged, for in due time, God will come through for them and their families. Dr. Cheggeh gives us solid scriptural interpretations on this topic that serve as a great guide to the ongoing search of the proper way to lay a right foundation for a righteous legacy to be inherited by future generations.

The pages of this book are filled to the brim with wisdom, knowledge, and encouragement which will lead everyone that is willing to follow its teachings to successfully leave behind a strong righteous legacy that will benefit and impact future generations. Without reservation, and with great joy, I highly recommend this book to every leader and to every believer.

—REV. DR. JOSEPH G. NJOROGE
HEAD, DEAPRTMENT OF HISTORY & POLITICAL SCIENCE,
ABRAHAM BALWIN STATE COLLEGE/
UNIVERSITY OF GEORGIA SYSTEM
CHAIRMAN BOARD OF TRUSTEES,
KENYA CHRISTIAN FELLOWSHIP IN AMERICA.
MEMBER OF BOARD OF TRUSTEES, NEEMA GOSPEL CHURCH.

Bishop, Dr. Armstrong Kamau Cheggeh is a man of vision and great influence. I am privileged to serve under him in the Fountain of Life Churches, International. I have had many opportunities to travel with him around the world to preach and train church leaders. He has mentored me, as well as hundreds of young leaders; encouraging them to go further in ministry and studies.

The success of a leader is in training and empowering other leaders to become the best they can be in the calling that the Lord has called them. I believe that Bishop Cheggeh's success will be seen in the lives of hundreds of us serving under him and the thousands of people he touches every year. He is leaving behind a righteous legacy to each and every one of these leaders.

The book you hold in your hands is a living testimony of a great man of faith who has worked tirelessly for over forty years to impact generations for Jesus. His favorite words and I quote, "I don't pray to live a long life, although that would be good, but that my life will impact others for Jesus every single day that I am alive." This book is written with great wisdom and knowledge, and has many practical lessons. I highly recommend it to all believers, and especially to the Christian leaders.

—PASTOR JOSEPH KAMAU
DIRECTOR OF EDUCATION
FOUNTAIN OF LIFE CHURCHES, INT'L

It is a great privilege and honor to have been accorded this rare opportunity to endorse this great book by my spiritual Mentor, Bishop Dr. Armstrong Cheggeh.

Dr. Cheggeh's book *Leaving Behind a Righteous Legacy*, delves into real day to day issues that are faced by all people irrespective of their standing in society and who realize that they have a God-given destiny to live. It also follows closely his book *Developing Relationships with Integrity*, which was released a few years back, and has been a blessing to thousands.

I came to know Dr. Cheggeh over fifteen years ago when I visited him at his office in Nairobi. We shared many issues pertaining to ministry challenges. During that season my family and I were going through tumultuous times on matters relating to the ministry and the Kingdom of God. I had just gone through some very painful experiences that I had never experienced in my Christian life. The betrayal of close ministry associates usually gets you into the "valley experiences," discussed in chapter two of this book. Bishop Cheggeh and his family in their traditional and accommodative spirit came in hardy and opened the doors of their lives and ministry to us. This gave us a sigh of relief to move on in the service of the Lord.

I am now proud to be serving under this able and gifted man

of God. He is a man of repute, a great scholar and a man who loves God very much. In his work, he cuts with ease through tribal, cultural, denominational and even other social economic barriers as he seeks to serve the Lord and the body of Christ.

It is against this backdrop that I highly acclaim and endorse this book as a very practical exposition and a must read by all servants of God including professionals, business people, students and even politicians, who aspire to leave behind something positive to their communities. Some of these leaders are aspiring for this very thing– to leave a strong, enduring legacy. Here then is the book that all in positions of leadership need.

In this book, one finds a lot of practical and useful substance that resonate quite well with what these leaders are going through and would help them easily navigate critical issues of life without necessarily rediscovering the wheel as it were!

In my own assessment, this book is purely an embodiment and a living testimony of the practical life the man of God is leading – indeed I see it as his personal testimony put in pen and paper for all of us to emulate in our quest to leave a righteous legacy that each of us dreams about. Bishop Cheggeh is helping us to clearly visualize what Apostle Paul meant when he said "–you are our epistle written in our hearts, known and read of all men…" (11 Corinthians 3:2)

—BISHOP SOLOMON W. WAWERU
GENERAL SECRETARY, FOUNTAIN OF LIFE CHURHCES INT'L

Bishop Dr. Armstrong Cheggeh is one of Kenya's most respected leaders in Evangelical circles. He is a pastor, an author and a frequent speaker at Marriages enrichment conferences, and Bible Seminars throughout Africa, India and United States of America.

I consider Bishop Armstrong to be one of the most remarkable Christian leaders that I have personally known over the years. His preaching and written work has helped to lay the foundation for one of the greatest moves of God in Africa and now in United States of America among the Kenyan Diaspora

Churches. Bishop Armstrong has founded and is helping to oversee more than 300 churches through his Fountain of Life Churches. His depth and sound biblical truths and godly wisdom as well as his daring faith in God has impacted many lives.

Bishop Armstrong is a spiritual father to many through his genuine humility and preference of others. This is demonstrated by the way he has instilled godly values into his children and given them a sense of good work ethics. He continues to build a rich legacy of faithfulness and hard work to everyone he encounters.

This book "Leaving Behind a Righteous Legacy" will help many to navigate through the process of passing on the baton from one generation to another and aligning God-Centered families. Leaving a godly Legacy should be the purpose of all parents. It is mandated in Scripture. Our most important job is to teach our children about the Lord and make it a priority. A Godly legacy begins when parents become intentional about creating a home that honors God.

—REV. JACKSON KING'ORI
SENIOR PASTOR, NEEMA GOSPEL CHURCH
DALLAS, TX.

Dedication

TO MY WIFE RHODA: You are indeed a Proverbs 31 woman. For thirty-five years, your love and support has been more than any man would ask for. My love and appreciation for you has grown with the years. Thanks you for your encouragement as I wrote this book.

To our family: Collins and Hannah, Clarence and Natasha, Casper, Celletine, and Cornelius. You are all so special to Daddy. When I think of my legacy, you are the first people that come to mind.

To my grandchildren: Ella, Ian, and Lilah. You'll never know how proud Grandpa is for each of you.

To the Family Glory Families: Each of your families has been such a blessing and support to us. I pray that each of you will leave a great legacy in your family, church, and community.

To Mike and Lois Njenga: You have been a great support over the years. Thanks for being faithful friends and prayer partners. You've been such a great support to the Kenyan community in the Seattle area.

To the leadership of the Fountain of Life Churches, International in Kenya, Uganda, Tanzania, Rwanda, Burundi, Congo, Zambia and India. I appreciate your unity and your support for each other as we continue serving the Lord together.

To the leadership of the Marriage Dynamics National Forum. Each of you has been such a blessing and an encouragement as we have served the Lord together over the last five years.

To all my spiritual sons and daughters. You are my legacy! You are my joy and crown. How I pray that each of you will leave a righteous legacy that will impact many lives to the honor and glory of our Lord.

To Hallee and Gregg Bridgeman. What a God-send you were! I really appreciate all you have done for me in getting this book published. What a legacy of compassion and brotherly love!

To each of you that is reading this book. My prayer is that this book will enhance your spiritual walk so that you, too, will leave a righteous legacy to your descendants and to those you encounter every day.

Table of Contents

LEAVING BEHIND A RIGHTEOUS LEGACY	i
COPYRIGHT NOTICE	ii
Endorsements	v
Dedication	xv
Table of Contents	xvii
Preface	xxv
Introduction	xxvii
Chapter 1	1
Being on God's Side	1
Why Caleb?	3
What Legacy Is	4
Landmark	4
God's Testimony	5
Pleasing the Lord	7
Caleb – He Stood out for God	8
Opposition by fellow Believers	10
God's Commendation is Better	11
Do not fuel the Flames Unnecessarily	13
Leadership Calls for Responsibility	14
Walk by Faith, not by Sight	15

God is on our Side	17
Faith: A Primary Key	17
Lessons from Chapter 1	19
Chapter 2	**21**
Being bold in our Walk	21
Taking Risk	21
Stability in spite of The Risks	23
A Place of greater Glory	25
Greater Glory from the Valley Experience	25
Called to life of Courage	26
Fear: An Enemy to Faith	27
You inherit what you Say	28
Say what He says – God's very Words	28
Line up with His will and Purpose	29
You are Precious	29
Words for Necessary Edification	32
Words Matter	33
Swear words and Curse Words	34
Lessons from Chapter 2	39
Chapter 3	**41**
Fear is a Snare	41
The Flight Mode	42
The Freeze Mode	45
The Attack Mode	50
Serving in Obscurity	52

God's approval should be our Focus	54
Waiting upon the Lord	55
Lessons from Chapter 3	57
Chapter 4	**59**
Standing Firm In Times Of Opposition	59
Whatever is not of Faith is Sin	60
Not by human Wisdom	61
In the Wilderness for foo Long	63
Godly Sorrow	64
Consideration for others	68
Shared Victory, Shared Joy	68
Each of us Counts	70
Settling Gradually	71
The Fullness of Time	71
Lesson from Chapter 4	75
Chapter 5	**77**
What Kind of Legacy: A Curse or a Blessing?	77
These Three left a Bad Legacy	77
The Man of God Who Left Debts	77
A Man that was cursed by a Whole Village	80
Died to no one's Sorrow	82
Two People with Outstanding Luminous Legacies	83
A Life that impacted Many Generations	86
Lessons from Chapter 5	93
Chapter 6	**95**

In Search of True Friends	95
Jesus the Faithful Friend	96
Giving and Sacrifice	98
Faithful Friends	100
The Absalom's Syndrome: The Sin of Betrayal	100
Forgiveness and Betrayal	102
Betrayed by a Close Friend	103
Friendship SpoilersBad Counsel	104
Above Petty Arguments	105
Viral Friends	105
Reconciling Friends	106
Lessons from Chapter 6	113
Chapter 7	115
God's Renewing Power	115
Strong For War	115
Change of Language	117
The Language of Faith	117
The Knowledge of God	119
Give me this Mountain!	121
A Life full of Passion	122
The Habitation of the Giants	123
Your Unconquered Territory	124
Lessons from Chapter 7	125
Chapter 8	127
Children: A Blessed Heritage	127

Respect for both Husband and Father	128
Confidence Gained from Up-Bringing	129
Claiming the Right Things	130
The Prayer that Gets Answered	131
Openness to Children	132
Do not Provoke your Children to Wrath	134
Calling for Change and Balance	135
Begin "Cultivation" Early	136
Make time for the Children	136
Spanking "Spare not the Rod"	137
Restricted Privileges	138
Withdrawal and Expulsion	139
Praise Your Children	140
Concern for future Generations	140
Lessons from Chapter 8	143
Chapter 9	145
Raise up the Foundation for many Generations (Part 1)	145
God's Word deeper than our finite Minds	147
Isaiah Chapter Fifty-Eight	147
Cry aloud!	149
Repentance is foundational	149
They Never gave Up	151
A Holy God	152
He Knows our Frame	153
Divine Invitation	153

A Broken and Contrite Heart 154
    Lesson from Chapter 9 157

Chapter 10 159
    Raising the Foundation for Many Generations (Part 2) 159

The Right way to Fast 160

Power of Prayer and Fasting 160

Power over Demonic Forces 161

Not for Strive and Debate 164

Fasting for Show! 165

Joint Prayer and Fasting 166

All Great Warriors Fast 167

Fasting and Repentance 168

Absolute or Complete Fasting 169

Regular or Normal Fasting 170

Partial Fasting – The Daniel's Fast 170

Purposes of Fasting 171

A word of Advice to Church Leaders 171

Faith that Works 173

Another Faith 174

Drawn by God 175

Physical and Social Needs 176

Ministry to the Whole Person 178

Plea for Widows 179

What can we do? 181

The Sooner the Better 182

    Retirement Funds 183
        Lessons from Chapter 10 187
Chapter 11 189
        Repentance brings Healing 189
    Impact on other People 190
    God's Grace 190
    Called to Intercede 191
    Sin of Prayerlessness 192
    Empty Religion 193
    The Motive Matters 194
    Oppression of Workers 194
    Importance of a Living Testimony 197
    Any Unforgivable Sins? 199
        Lessons From Chapter 11 203
Conclusion: What I Leave Behind Matters 205
Bibliography 211
About the Author 217
Contact the Author 218

Armstrong Cheggeh

Preface

BISHOP DR. ARMSTRONG CHEGGEH'S book, "Leaving Behind a Righteous Legacy" focuses on Kingdom living. This is a holistic vision that transforms present and future generations to live for the glory of God. Dr. Cheggeh demonstrates, in a very passionate and pastoral way, how the body of Christ in the 21st century can live victoriously and in an uncompromising way in the light of eternity. Throughout this engaging book he emphasizes the need for believers to live in such a way as to honor God in every detail of their lives so that they establish a righteous legacy for posterity.

The central figure in this book is Caleb of old, a godly and exemplary man in his generation, who followed God whole-heartedly into the Promised Land. Bishop Cheggeh unravels how Caleb's uncompromising faith, courage, and spirit, separated him from his generation and thus providing a lasting legacy for his family and the people of God. Dr. Cheggeh challenges believers everywhere, and especially Christian leaders, to stand firm even in the midst of trials and opposition. He exhorts believers to view these difficult seasons as opportunities to mold and bless God's faithful servants. The Lord elevates his devoted servants, who choose to endure these hardships and trials, to greater heights of glory and blessing. Dr. Cheggeh emphasizes the best place for believers, during these times of opposition and challenges, is not in self-made comfort zones but in the center of God's will for their lives.

This timely book is a call for Christians to stand firm on God's promises and not to walk in fear and doubt, thus missing His best plan for our lives, as did the ten Hebrew spies. Our main goal, according to Dr. Cheggeh, should not just be to live long lives but to discover and walk in God's will no matter the circumstance or opposition.

Dr. Cheggeh advises believers to spend quality time in God's word and constant prayer in order to discern God's voice and to find a place of spiritual stability and intimacy with our heavenly Father.

Dr. Cheggeh prophetically reminds us that the victorious Christian life has no short cuts but is entered by only those who, like Caleb, choose to pursue God with their whole heart.

—REV. DR. PATRICK G. KIHIU, PhD.
CHAPLAIN US ARMY
FOUNDER, KIHIU INT'L MINISTRIES, INC. (USA)

Introduction

A FEW YEARS AGO I was doing my personal devotions when a certain verse caught my attention. In Numbers 14:24, God says of Caleb, the son of Jephuneh, "But My servant Caleb, because he has a different spirit in him and has followed me fully, I will bring into the land where he went, and his descendants shall inherit it." The words, "and his descendants shall inherit it," jumped out at me! The word indeed became *a rhema* word to me–a very timely word that spoke to my situation in that particular moment. It ministered to the core of my being.

As I meditated on the words of this verse, I realized that the blessing God was promising Caleb was much bigger than himself and would outlive him. Long after Caleb's life in Canaan his descendants would enjoy God's blessings and prosperity because of Caleb's faithfulness. As I have written later in this book, some of his descendants would say, "were it not for "grandpa" Caleb we would not be where we are today." (p. 7).

As I began thinking of Caleb's life, especially reading about his life forty-five years after settling in Canaan (Joshua 14:6-12), the subject of legacy came to mind. I felt that the Lord wanted to remind me of the need to live in such a way that I would leave an enduring righteous legacy behind. I also felt impressed to share this message with others. I called the message, "Leaving Behind a Righteous Legacy." The more I preached on this theme, the more I felt that this message needed to be heard by the greater Christian community. I then began writing several articles on the theme of Legacy in the Revival Springs magazine.

This book is the fulfilment of the dream of getting this message to the greater body of Christ. I pray that it will help you, the reader, become a better steward of your life and everything that the Lord has entrusted to you. God expects of each of us to leave behind a legacy of blessing to our descendants. Our lives should not be lived just for ourselves, but for the Lord and His great kingdom.

Paul tells the believers in Philippians to work out their own salvation with fear and trembling (Philippians 2:12). As I wrote this book my experience was with, "fear and trembling," especially as I meditated more on the subject at hand. My initial thought especially when I began writing this book was, "O my goodness, who can really qualify to write such a book?"

However, the more I thought about it, the more I was reminded of God's marvelous grace because indeed there is nothing that qualifies any of us to hold any position of leadership or do anything in His kingdom, but for His marvelous and boundless grace and mercy. Like Paul, I can say with all confidence that I have not made it yet, but I do press on believing that as I continue to depend upon God's grace am being changed to be the kind of man God wants me to be. I also believe that the little I have invested in my own family, as well as in the thousands of lives our ministry has touched over the years will amount to some kingdom investment and establish a lasting legacy that will remain long after I am gone.

I pray that as you read this book it will change you just as it changed me as I wrote it. I found myself repeatedly pausing in my writing to consider what kind of legacy I would leave to both my family and ministry. This book challenges every believer to live every day of their lives with eternity in their minds. The book calls every child of God to have a kingdom mindset–living to impact others for Christ and to honor and glorify God every day of their lives, realizing that whatever we say or do today will indeed impact our future generations. My personal and ministry life changed as I wrote this book and more so as I re-read it in preparation for publication.

My prayer is that the Holy Spirit will use this book to touch you, the reader and cause you to consider what legacy you will leave behind to your family, church, and community.

Armstrong Cheggeh
Nicholasville, Kentucky
http://folcinternational.com

> *Our lives should not be lived just for ourselves, but for the Lord and His great kingdom.*

Armstrong Cheggeh

Chapter 1

Being on God's Side

WHEN YOU READ the book of Numbers, you come across these names: Shammua, Shaphat, Igal, Palti, Gaddiel, Gaddi, Ammiel, Sethur, Nahbi, and Geuel.

If you are an average Christian you do not even know who these men were. Actually, you probably do not know anybody named after them. Do you know of anybody in the Christian community named Igal, Sethur, and Geuel? Probably not, and yet these were very special leaders in Israel. These were the other ten spies who accompanied Joshua and Caleb. The believing community over the centuries determined not only to forget these guys, so much so, that they do not name their children after them!

On the other hand, how many people do you know named Joshua or Caleb? Of course we all know someone named after these two great leaders. The reason we use the names of these two great men to this day is because they chose to do that which was right and they left a legacy of faith that we can emulate.

The difference between the other cowardly spies and these faithful servants of God became very evident upon their return from spying out the land of Canaan. Caleb's faith in God, his determination, and resolve to be and do that which was right whatever the cost elevated him to a place whereby even God Himself would give a testimony of his life.

> *"But my servant Caleb, because he has a different spirit in him and has followed me fully, I will bring into the land where he went, and his descendants shall inherit it"* (Numbers 14:24).

These other leaders qualified in that each was a top leader in his own tribe. However, they failed in God's standards for leadership. Just because someone qualifies in worldly standards does not necessarily mean they will qualify in God's service. Allen observes, "That they were each leaders of their tribe did not guarantee that they were adequate for the leadership role God desired they would have." (The Expositor, 804).

> **When compared to eternity, our lives on earth are extremely short, and yet what we say, do, or think impacts both ur future lives on earth, as well as the lives of of every person with whom we interact.**

When compared to eternity, our lives on earth are extremely short, and yet what we say, do, or think impacts both our future lives on earth, as well as the lives of every person we interact with. We cannot then afford to be careless with how we live on earth because it will really affect and impact other people and has implications on our eternal destiny. I think we cannot talk of having a powerful, enduring legacy without talking about walking with God. Life without God makes no sense, and a life lived without God is a wasted life.

In Exodus 32, Moses the servant of the Lord was greatly aggravated by Dothan, Korah and Abiram. In this epochal moment in the history of the young nation of Israel, Moses asked the people to choose whom they would follow (Exodus 32:26). Neutrality was out of question; there are no neutral places when it comes to serving the Lord. Those who opposed Moses received immediate retribution. Through this and many other lessons in the wilderness, the Lord showed the nation of Israel that beyond any shadow of a doubt He would not accept second place. He is, was, and will always be a jealous God. He alone is God and cannot share His glory with any other. He deserves and demands total commitment and whole-hearted service from His people.

God punishes disobedience but always abundantly blesses those who walk in faith and obedience. The Psalmist reminds us that God always has good things prepared for those who honor Him. "Oh, how great *is* Your goodness, which You have laid up for those who fear You, which You have prepared for those who trust in You in the presence of the sons of men! (Psalm 31:19).

Why Caleb?

There are a number of people in the Bible that I could have chosen to follow regarding the subject of legacy, but I have chosen to follow the life of one of my favorite characters in the Word of God. His name was Caleb, the son of Jephunneh. Interestingly, even though he eventually proved to be a much more effective and lasting leader than the other ten spies who went to spy out the land of Canaan, he began just like any of the others. There was nothing so special or particular about him. He was appointed by Moses to be among the twelve spies that would go and spy out the land of Canaan. All we know is that he was the leader of the tribe of Judah (Numbers 13:6).

According to Numbers 14:24, Caleb's faithfulness would not only benefit him, his wife, and his immediate children; it would also benefit all his future generations. God said that whatever Caleb would inherit would eventually become a blessing to his descendants. He was going to leave behind a lasting legacy. He was going to leave something that would forever bless anybody associated with him. This is why I chose to discuss the life of Caleb. The emphasis in this book is: Do not live just for yourself. When you leave this world, let it be said that you left a legacy that blessed all your future generations. Let it be said that your life blessed someone else and prompted them to live better lives. Let it be said that your life lifted someone else to the next level. When someone has lived in the will of God they always impact other people around them for the better.

What Legacy Is

Since I am talking about leaving behind an enduring righteous legacy, let me first explain what a legacy is. A legacy is something handed down from an ancestor or a predecessor or just something passed on from the past. In historical terms, a legacy is something that is handed down from one period of time to another period of time. (Brown, 1561). A historical legacy can be a positive thing or a negative thing. Someone can leave a very negative impact on his future generations or something that will benefit them even to the tenth generation. In the case of Caleb, his legacy was going to bless all his future generations.

Some families pass objects and ideas down from generation to generation. These objects and ideas can also be called legacies. A legacy may have to do with one person or many people. Thus legacies can be left by an individual, a group of people, a tribe, or even a nation.

When you talk of "Legacy," words like, heritage, birthright, inheritance, endowment, or landmarks, come to mind.

Landmark

When we talk of landmarks and legacies, we mean the kind of imprint or impact that someone leaves behind that affects others in his family, tribe, and nation. Each of us leaves some landmarks or legacies wherever we go, whether we know it or not and whether we like it or not. None of us can escape it. It is not a question of if you have a legacy or a landmark to leave behind; it is a question of what kind of legacy or landmark you will leave. Your strengths and values do leave a mark on those who you encounter every single day of your life.

Knowing this should make every child of God walk very carefully because whatever you say or do does affect someone else. Even as you read this book, whatever you are involved in whether in words or actions is not neutral. Our words and actions have ripple effects whether we acknowledge it or not. They have a positive or negative impact on someone else.

God's Testimony

"But my servant Caleb, because he has a different spirit in him and has followed me fully, I will bring into the land where he went, and his descendants shall inherit it" (Numbers 14:24).

First I stress a very important aspect in the life of this great man of God. Note from our scriptural passage that God Himself commends the life and ministry of Caleb. How awesome that God Himself would testify to someone's greatness in the faith. In most African Evangelical or Charismatic circles we have something called a personal testimony. When we gather together for fellowship or even when we meet with friends, we like to share our testimonies. We talk of what the Lord has done in us and for us.

This indeed is a great spiritual tradition where we emphasize the power of God's Hand and His greatness in our lives. The Psalmist tells us to "make known His deeds among the peoples...talk of all His wondrous works" (Psalm 105:1-2). However, it is one thing to talk of His wondrous works and another thing to have God Himself talking about our wondrous works! Can you imagine the Lord Himself talking about how great and faithful you have been in your vocation or ministry? That's exactly what happened in the life of Caleb. The Lord was so pleased by Caleb's ways that He testified about him. I love to testify about the Lord's Hand in my life, but what a joy it would be for Him to testify about my service for Him!

It is much better to seek God's approval than the approval of men. Jesus told His disciples, "And do not fear those who kill the soul, but rather fear Him who is able to destroy both soul and body in hell" (Matthew 10:28). I desire above all else to have God's approval in my life and ministry. All other approvals become secondary to my Heavenly Father's "Well done thou good and faithful servant." I hope and pray that we are not waiting to hear these great words at the judgment seat of Christ (See 11 Corinthians 5:10, Matthew 25:20-23), but rather that each of us is living to hear these words in our spirits each and every day of our lives. Doesn't the scriptures not say that, "the Spirit Himself bears witness with our spirits that we are children of God?" (Romans 8:16). May the same Spirit bear witness with our spirits that we are living in accordance to God's will and purpose for our lives.

The intimacy of such a relationship is great and to be desired, and at the same time it is a great challenge. The great British preacher John Stott reminds church leaders of this very thing; "However, if on the one hand it is a comforting thing to be accountable to Christ, on the other hand it is challenging, for his standards are high and holy. And though much of a Pastor's work is unseen and unsupervised by human beings, yet we are always in his presence" (*Basic Christian*, 103).

Being in His presence constantly is such a joyful and empowering experience. It is also a humbling experience to think that the God of all creation accommodates Himself into such finite and feeble beings that we are. However, there is no better place for us to be than to be in the presence of our loving heavenly Father.

Pleasing the Lord

The apostle Paul says, "Therefore we make it our aim, whether present or absent, to be well pleasing to Him" (2 Corinthians 5:9). Paul found the aspect of pleasing the Lord as the key to our spiritual life. Caleb likewise walked in such a way that the Lord testified to the fact he had pleased Him. It is important that our aim in life be to please the Lord above all else. It is okay to do your best to please the people the Lord has placed with or over you in the ministry. There is definitely a place for the honor we accord to our pastors, presbyters, overseers, and bishops, but we need to watch out that none of those honors come anywhere close to the honor we have for our Master.

The Lord says, "I am the Lord, that is my name; and my glory I will not give to another, nor my praise to carved images" (Isaiah 42:8). God does not share His glory with any man however great they rise in ministry. This is why the first century believers challenged the status quo in the religious hierarchy, "But Peter and John answered and said to them, whether it is right in the sight of God to listen to you more that to God, you judge. (Acts 4:19). To these early believers it was so important that they did not dishonor the name of the Lord in order to gain men's approval. May God give us the grace to stand our ground when we are tempted to compromise our stand and give greater honor to religious hierarchies or particular leaders.

When Caleb honored and pleased the Lord at the entry into the land of promise, the Lord made sure that this would not be the end of his story. He says in the verse we read earlier, "I will bring into the land where he went, and his descendants shall inherit it." God would bring Caleb into the land of promise, but not just for himself. He would bring him so that in as much as he would inherit the land, all his future generations would also benefit from his faithfulness to God and His call upon his life. All of Caleb's future generations would look back and say, if it were not for "grandpa" Caleb we would not be where we are today. What a legacy! Let that be your dream. Let that be your prayer.

Let that be your life.

Caleb – He Stood out for God

As previously stated, Caleb is one of my favorite Biblical characters. I like the way the Lord spoke of this great Warrior, "But my servant Caleb because he has a different spirit" (Numbers 14:24).

God spoke of Caleb as a man with a "different spirit." That is key to understanding the subject we are pursuing in this chapter. You cannot be greatly used of God until you come to a place in your spiritual life where you are willing to literally stand out for God in the midst of the forces that would want you to blend in. That is usually easily said than done. It is very hard to stand alone, especially when it is unpopular to do so. Most of the times we like siding with those things that are politically correct even in the church. Amy Carmichael, who was a missionary to India said, "Better, far better walk with God in the dark than walk alone in the light" (*This One*, 65).

When Caleb stood out for God he almost paid with his own life for having, "a different spirit." It is not always easy when you choose to follow God's way. There are times that He may call you to stand all alone and sometimes completely against the tide.

Paul and Peter talked about the peculiarity we need to have as believers. Paul says, "Therefore, 'Come out from among them and be separate, says the Lord. Do not touch what is unclean, and I will receive you. I will be a Father to you, and you shall be my sons and daughters, says the Lord almighty.'" (2 Corinthians 6:17). Peter says, "But you are a chosen generation a royal priesthood, a holy nation, His own special people, that you may proclaim the praises of Him who has called you out of darkness into His marvelous light." (1 Peter 2:9).

Our heavenly Father expects His children to continually manifest His glory to the people around them. He works with His people to strengthen and renew them constantly, so that they do not depend upon past victories and glory, but rather on His continuing work within their spirits. Of this renewing experience, Ron Rand says, "God does not provide reruns of last year's religious experience. God is living and his work is new every morning" (*For Fathers*, 170).

God's call for His people in the Old Testament and into the New Testament was for them to live holy and separated lives. God would not entertain worldliness or the influence of other faiths or religions among His people. This, of course does not mean living a monastic life, although indeed there are times you may feel the need to separate yourself even from friends and family for a while to seek God's will for yourself or for the ministry He has entrusted to you. However, the separation we are talking about means living in such a way that the ways of the world do not influence how you live out your life. Our brother John tells us, "Do not love the world or the things in the world. If anyone loves the world, the love of the Father is not in him" (1 John 2:15).

> *This separation does not mean we should not deal with unbelievers at all because that would mean that we would have to get out of this world.*

This separation does not mean we should not deal with unbelievers at all because that would mean that we would have to get out of this world. Jesus prayed about this very issue in his High Priestly prayer, "I do not pray that you should take them out of the world, but that you should keep them from the evil one" (John 17:15). The idea here is that even though we will live in this world, we have to live to the honor and glory of His great Name. That is how our brother Caleb lived and received great commendation, not just from some godly person, or some senior religious leader, but from God Himself.

If Jesus prayed for the Father to keep us while in this world, then it is possible to remain strong and walk in Him; in spite of all the challenges that come our way as we live the Christian life in this world. God's Hand will keep and guide us. God's promise is that He will never leave us nor forsake us (Hebrews 13:5). What a joy to know that, "He who keeps you will not slumber. Behold, He who keeps Israel shall neither slumber nor sleep" (Psalm 121:3-4).

The most important and encouraging thing in life is to know that God himself promises to work within us to make us what He wants us to be. This divine intervention is continuous and goes on throughout our earthly lives. Calvin Miller, a very prominent scholar and preacher strongly opposes the idea that our spiritual journey can be accomplished in one spiritual encounter with the Divine. He says, "I haven't much patience with people who believe that God is so trivial that all that he is may be encountered in one single moment of being saved. Rather his glory much comes gradually into fragile, finite lives or we would die overwhelmed by his immensity" (*Into the Depth*, 109). The idea here is that God, through the process of sanctification works in us by His word, by His Spirit and by Christian fellowship and ministry to make us what He wants us to be. He works not in a moment of time, but rather throughout our lives, both to will and to do for His good pleasure (Philippians 2:13)

Opposition by fellow Believers

"And all the congregation said to stone them with stones. Now the glory of the Lord appeared in the tabernacle of meeting Before all the children of Israel" (Numbers 14:10).

We must understand that Caleb was not standing against the pagans and heathens of his day. No. He stood out against fellow "believers" (See Numbers 14:6-10). Standing up against the ungodliness outside the church is sometimes easier because in such situations you have part or the whole church behind you. However, when you choose to stand above the petty politics, the gossip, the immorality, and all kinds of compromised standards in the church, then you are in for trouble! Most often the majority of church people find it much easier to remove the speck in other people's eyes, and find it really difficult to even acknowledge, let alone remove the plank in their own eyes (See Matthew 7:4-5).

Such was the case in Caleb's story. Nobody would have opposed him if he had decried the evils among Amorites, Hittites, Perizzites, Canaanites, Hivites, and Jebusites. Of course everybody would have agreed that those were great sinners! The "Amens" would have rang loud and clear. However, when Caleb's and Joshua's testimony differed from the other ten spies, they were in for big trouble. The people talked of stoning them to death! (Numbers 14:10). They almost paid with their lives for standing for God on that day.

God's Commendation is Better

Caleb received God's commendation and blessing for choosing to stand alone for God in the face of great opposition. The same kind of blessing will come upon such people as will choose to honor and defend God's name in the face of challenge or opposition. There are times that the Lord will call us to stand alone even within the confines of the church. Throughout church history God has raised men and women who had to learn to stand against the tide and defend God's honor.

Even though future generations have sometimes honored those great men and women, they often did not receive recognition and praise from their own generations. Individuals like Martin Luther, William Wilberforce, Florence Nightingale, Polycarp, John Huss, St. Francis of Assisi, and many others like them who "obtained a good testimony through faith" (Hebrews 11:39), and yet did not live to see the results of their stand in the midst of opposition. These are they that will receive the divine commendation during the judgment seat of Christ, "Well done thou good and faithful servant" (Matthew 25:20-23). However, during their lives, each of these did not know how much their lives impacted future generations. They did not choose men's applause or praise. They did not live for self-promotion, self-praise, and self-aggrandizement. They lived to honor and glorify the Lord, though not being acknowledged or recognized by their peers or their generations.

It is important to note that in the bible days, as well as in church history the majority of the people did not accept or appreciate those who spoke for God. These preachers and prophets were lonely voices most of the time. The greater body of believers often rejected and even ridiculed their work. The greater majority of the nation of Israel rejected most prophets in the Old Testament, like Ezekiel, Jeremiah, Amos, and many other prophets.

Most of the political and religious leaders of the day opposed the prophets and in the case of Jeremiah they tried to have him killed on a number of occasions (Jeremiah 26:8-9, 38:4-6). These prophets spoke for God when everybody else wanted to respect the status quo. Do not be surprised that this opposition does happen to this day. I have experienced this kind of opposition from the very people I had expected the greatest support. My most painful experiences did not come from outside the church, but from people who were in the very fellowship of churches I belonged to. In my book, *Developing Relationships with Integrity*, I emphasized that even though opposition and challenges will come our way, as believers we have to practice the love of Christ and forbearance and rejoice in spite of it all (Cheggeh, 83). We cannot allow the situations around us or the opposition we face to determine how we live or the attitudes we will have in life. The joy of the Lord needs to be our strength even in times of challenge (See Nehemiah 8:10).

Sometimes when God is preparing us for great roles in His kingdom, He first allows us to go through fire, so that He can mold us into the shape he wants. Henry and Claude Blackaby explain this divine principle. "God has to lay some basic foundations in your life before He can prepare you for the larger tasks (*Experiencing God*, 117). We all need to be ready for this preparatory work. God knows our frame and prepares us accordingly. Sometimes this work will take longer in some of us than in others depending on what our all-knowing heavenly Father wants to make of us.

Do not fuel the Flames Unnecessarily

Even though I am discussing the issue of opposition, I would caution the average believer against living in such a way as to attract opposition. We are not called to cause or attract opposition. Apostle Peter admonishes the believers to be careful that they are not opposed for being careless in their spiritual walk. "But let none of you suffer as a murderer, a thief, an evildoer, or as a busybody in other people's matters. Yet if anyone suffers as a Christian, let him not be ashamed, but let him glorify God in this matter" (1 Peter 4:15-16).

There are times that we suffer because of our own foolishness and carelessness. In such times we cannot claim to be suffering for Christ. If anything we may be suffering for our own misguided spirituality. I have known of brothers who have suffered because of their own carelessness in school or their place of work, and then they turn around and claim to be suffering for Christ. No one should ever make such claims when indeed they are suffering for their own carelessness. Even in my own life, I have had seasons when I suffered because of my own carelessness and because I acted unwisely. Such suffering cannot be called "suffering for Christ."

Such was not the suffering in Caleb's life. He stood for God when God's honor was at stake in the nation of Israel. The Lord needed someone to stand on His side and found only these two faithful men – Joshua and Caleb.

It is easier to serve and indeed to rejoice in the Lord when everything is going on well. The test of our faith is normally not when things are flowing smoothly but more in time of storms. "My brethren, count it all joy when you fall into various trials, knowing that the testing of your faith produces patience." (James 1:2). Job also proclaimed that after the testing of his faith he would come out as gold (Job 23:10). Most often when our faith is tested, if we choose to stand for God, then our faith is strengthened and polished by the experience.

Our brother, Wesley Duewel, suggests that sometimes when we are tested it can become a testimony to the world. "God may even permit you to pass through difficult experiences in order to prove to non-Christians that Christ is real and that you are genuine" (*Ablaze*, 169). In times of great persecution there are many who come to Christ by just observing how faithful the Christians are during the testing of their faith. That's what happened in the early church. Multitudes were won to Christ by just observing the steadfastness and faith of the martyrs.

Leadership Calls for Responsibility

At Paran, God told Moses to send a leader from every tribe to spy out the land (Numbers 13:2; 14:6-8). Apparently each of the twelve spies was a qualified leader, since it is unlikely that Moses would have sent unqualified people on such a sensitive mission. These were his chief commandos, and yet ten of them when put the test proved to be dismal failures.

Moses, at this point had already received advice from Jethro, his father-in-law on the kind of leaders to choose. He taught Moses to practice the art of delegation. It is most likely that each of these twelve leaders was chosen according to the four qualifications endorsed by Jethro (Exodus 18:21):

Able men: Qualified to do what they had to do.

Such as fear God: Men who revered and followed God's way.

Men of truth: Honest, truthful, men of integrity.

Hating covetousness: Hating unjust gain.

It is interesting then how men of such caliber would turn around and just do the opposite of what was expected of them. It seems that even though they had at one time proved to be capable leaders, something had gone wrong in how they judged issues in God's kingdom. Sometimes when leaders get to a certain level of leadership they forget how they got there. How often we have observed the same in church leadership. We have seen people that once served God with great passion, and who sought God's mind on every decision in their lives and ministry turning out to be men or women walking completely in the flesh. May all of us be reminded at all times that everything we are or hope to be, and everything we have is by the grace of God. You are what and where you are by His enabling hand.

Warren Wiersbe reminds the leaders to always be on the move. "Leaders must not stand still or they will go backward. They must keep moving ahead so that others can move with them and claim new territories" (47). A Christian leader should never get to a place where they feel that they have made it. Like Paul we should always press on towards the goal for the prize of the upward call of God in Christ Jesus" (Philippians 3:14). These other ten spies seem to have come to a place in their lives where God's values were not of importance in their decision making. May we ever be mindful of what the Lord would have us say or do, as we continue serving Him.

Joshua and Caleb understood their place and calling in God's kingdom. They pursued their calling to the best of their ability. According to Numbers 13:1-25, there was no way that anybody would have differentiated Joshua and Caleb from the other spies. All of them seemed to be very committed leaders as they left to spy out the land. The difference came when they began to report on the things that all of them had witnessed. Sometimes it is not what you see but rather how you see! It is great when we learn to see by the eyes of faith. Both Joshua and Caleb allowed God's spirit to control how they saw things. "For we walk by faith, not by sight (2 Corinthians 5:7).

Walk by Faith, not by Sight

There are times when your own sight and experience become your worst enemies. Indeed, experience is not always the best teacher; sometimes it is simply a faith destroyer. How often we have missed a great opportunity to trust in God's hand of deliverance because we depended on our past experiences. May the Lord teach us to walk by faith. When the Lord asks us to do a particular thing, it is not because He trusts in our ability to accomplish the task, but rather because He has the ability to enable us to accomplish the task. That way He still receives all the glory. Actually any time we feel inadequate to accomplish a particular task, it becomes yet another blessed opportunity for God to show Himself faithful to us one more time.

The ten spies got so wrapped up in the pragmatics of conquering the land that they took God out of the equation. They depended wholly on how they would do the conquest. They forgot one great lesson that all men and women of faith must learn. "The battle belongs to the Lord" (Exodus 14:14, 2 Chronicles 20:15). How often in our lives when faced with life-threatening challenges we take God out of the equation and take the matter into our own hands. Such was the fate of these ten spies. They saw themselves as tiny, little grasshoppers that would be easily defeated and crushed by the big giants (Numbers 13:33). Caleb and his friend Joshua saw it differently. They did not necessarily see themselves crushing the giants, but rather their God crushing the giants for them. God is still in the business of crushing any giants that come our way, but we have to learn to trust in Him. It is not a question of whether the Lord will do it, but rather whether we will trust Him to do it.

The ten spies made a mistake of walking by sight. This was one grievous mistake! It is most likely that the mighty men of Canaan were bigger in stature than the Israelites and thus the statement, "we were like grasshoppers." However, physical strength and military superiority is not an end in itself. These spies forgot an important lesson, which the Lord had already taught them as they left Egypt. Greatness of stature, expertise, and military might were no match to ***Jehovah Sabaoth!*** He has never lost a battle. Having the God of Israel on their side meant that they would always experience victory, however great the enemy was. They only needed to remember the words of Moses at the crossing of the Red Sea "Do not be afraid. Stand still, and see the salvation of the Lord, which He will accomplish for you today…" (Exodus 14:13).

God is on our Side

Caleb seems to have remembered this lesson when he declared, "Let us go up at once and take possession, for we are well able to overcome it" (Numbers 13:30). It seems that the statures and military strength of the Canaanites had not diluted his faith in God. Caleb believed that with God on your side, the size and number of enemies would be immaterial. This reminds us of the words of Jonathan the son of King Saul. When faced with the challenge of fighting the Philistines, he told his armor-bearer, "Come, let us go over to the garrison of these uncircumcised; it may be that the Lord will work for us. For nothing restrains the Lord from saving by many or by few." (1 Samuel 14:6). To Jonathan and Caleb, it really did not matter how many or how strong the enemy was. The most important thing was that the Lord was on their side. As you read this chapter, please be reminded of this same lesson: it really does not matter how great or powerful your enemy or battle in life is, our God is still greater than all the challenges that come your way. On this subject, the Apostle Paul, exclaimed, "What then shall we say to these things? If God *is* for us, who *can be* against us? (Romans 8:31). The idea here is that we are safe and secure when the Lord is on our side.

Faith: A Primary Key

The faith of both Caleb and Jonathan is something that each of us needs to have. We need to understand that the number and strength of our present-day enemies is inconsequential. Our God is immutable (See Malachi 3:6, Hebrews 13:8). His power and glory are changeless. Whatever battles come your way, you will need to be reminded that the God of Caleb and Jonathan is your God. He does not deal with us according to the strength and size of our enemies. He deals with us according to the faith we have in

Him. Our brother Wigglesworth reminds us of the power of faith. "Faith has the power to make you what God wants you to be; only you must be ready to step into the plan and believe His word" (Smith, 77).

Faith in God is all you need when facing the challenges in life. There is nothing too big or too unreachable for someone who has faith in God. Faith is the greatest weapon when facing any battle. Lindsay reminds us that faith encompasses every aspect of a believer's life. "Faith is the source of our strength, our provision, our courage, our guidance, and our victory over the world system, the flesh, and the Devil" (*Combat Faith*, 21). Wigglesworth calls faith the "power of limitless possibilities within the believer (*Smith*, 144).

Jesus told us, "Therefore I say to you, whatever things you ask when you pray believe that you receive them and you will have them" (Mark 11:24). Note that He uses the word, "whatever," meaning that faith in God has no limit. Our Lord used the similar wording when bidding farewell to His beloved disciples, "and whatever you ask in my name, that I will do, that the Father may be glorified in the Son. If you ask anything in my name, I will do it" (John 14:13).

The writer of Hebrews shows us the importance of faith: "But without faith it is impossible to please Him; for he who comes to God must believe that He is, and that He is a rewarder of those who diligently seek Him" (Hebrews 11:6). When you come to God and believe Him for Who he is, you can expect Him to fight for you when faced by any challenge in life. He still rewards those who diligently seek Him.

When I leave life on earth, I would most of all love to leave a legacy of faith in God. I want my descendants to know that I dared believe God even in the most trying of seasons. I want my family and my spiritual children to know that I believed God in order to lay for them a solid foundation upon which they too will build.

Lessons from Chapter 1

WHEN COMPARED TO eternity, our lives on earth are extremely short, and yet what we say, do, or think impacts both our future lives on earth, as well as the lives of every person with whom we interact.

Neutrality is out of question; there are no neutral places when it comes to serving the Lord.

God punishes disobedience, but always abundantly blesses those who walk in faith and obedience.

Each of us, whether we know it or not and whether we like it or not, do leave some landmarks or legacies wherever we go. None of us can escape it. It is not a question of if you have a legacy or a landmark to leave behind; it is a question of what kind of legacy or landmark you will leave.

It is one thing to talk of God's wondrous works and another thing to have Him talking about our wondrous works!

Being in His presence constantly is such a joyful and empowering experience. It is also a humbling experience to think that the God of all creation accommodates Himself into such finite and feeble beings that we are.

There is definitely a place for the honor we accord to our pastors, presbyters, overseers, and bishops, but we need to watch out that none of those honors come anywhere close to the honor we have for our Master.

You cannot be greatly used of God until you come to a place in your spiritual life where you are willing to literally stand out for God in the midst of the forces that would want you to blend in.

Our heavenly Father expects His children to continually manifest His glory to the people around them. He works with His people to strengthen and renew them constantly, so that they do not depend upon past victories and glory, but rather on His continuing work within their spirits.

The most important and encouraging thing is to know that God himself promises to work within us to make us what He wants us to be. This divine intervention is continuous and goes on throughout our earthly lives.

Sometimes when God is preparing us for great roles in His kingdom, He first does allow us to go through fire, so that He can mold us into the shape he wants.

There are times that we suffer because of our own foolishness and carelessness. In such times we cannot claim to be suffering for Christ. If anything we may be suffering for our own misguided spirituality.

At times your own sight and experience become your worst enemies. Indeed, experience is not always the best teacher; sometimes it is simply a faith destroyer.

God is still in the business of crushing any giants that come our way, but we have to learn to trust in Him. It is not a question of whether the Lord will do it, but rather whether we will trust Him to do it.

Whatever battles come your way, you will need to be reminded that the God of Caleb and Jonathan is your God. He does not deal with us according to the strength and size of our enemies. He deals with us according to the faith we have in Him.

Chapter 2

Being bold in our Walk

> "But Joshua the son of Nun and Caleb the son of Jephunneh, who were among those who had spied out the land, tore their clothes; and they spoke to all the congregation of the children of Israel, saying: "The land we passed through to spy out is an exceedingly good land. If the Lord delights in us, then He will bring us into this land and give it to us, 'a land which flows with milk and honey. Only do not rebel against the LORD, nor fear the people of the land, for they are our bread; their protection has departed from them, and the Lord is with us. Do not fear them." And all the congregation said to stone them with stones. Now the glory of the Lord appeared in the tabernacle of meeting before all the children of Israel" (Numbers 14:6-10).

Taking Risk

WHEN JOSHUA AND Caleb stood before a whole community that had turned against God and His word, they showed great courage. They did not waver even when the people picked up stones to kill them (Numbers 14:6). They stood firm on what they believed. They tried to persuade the people to follow God's will and even after the people had turned against the Lord, they showed the depth of their faith in God by tearing their clothes as a sign of pain, sorrow, and repentance on behalf of their fellow Israelites.

Of such true, effective, and lasting leaderships, our brother Myles Munroe says, "Leaders are willing to challenge tradition, experiment with new ideas and explore" (*Becoming*, 39). These words would rightly describe Caleb's life and ministry. He and his friend Joshua were leaders that were willing to explore the new, the unknown and the unfamiliar without fear as long as God was with them. They did not allow the unfamiliar to scare them like the rest of the spies. These two men were willing to go to places that they did not know as long as God was with them.

There is no challenge that is too risky when God is involved. There is no valley too dark when God's presence abides with us. This is what David may have meant when he said, "Better is one day in your courts than a thousand elsewhere; I would rather be a doorkeeper in the house of my God than dwell in the tents of the wicked (Psalm 84:10). In other words, "I would rather be in God's presence than be in the most comfortable of places or situations." The darkest and coldest of dungeons can be a place of real peace, when God's presence is abiding in an individual's life.

> The darkest and coldest of dungeons can be a place of real peace, when God's presence is abiding in an individual's life.

As you read this chapter, you might be going through the roughest of times. Just keep on believing and don't give up hope. Learn to dwell in God's presence even in seasons of storms. David said, "One thing I have desired of the Lord, that will I seek; that I may dwell in the house of the Lord all the days of my life. To behold the beauty of the Lord and to inquire in His temple (Psalm 27:4). In verse 5 of the same passage he gives the reason why it is important to dwell in God's presence. "For in the time of trouble He shall hide me in His pavilion; in the secret place of His tabernacle He shall hide me; He shall set me high upon a rock" (Psalm 27:5).

Stability in spite of The Risks

Often, the walk of faith requires that we learn to take risks. God does not promise an easy life. Any committed servant of God needs to understand that risking one's life is part and parcel of the mission God has entrusted us with. As Caleb accompanied other spies into the land of promise and later when facing the rebellion of the nation of Israel, he must have understood that serving God included taking risks. Both occasions called for stability in the face of great challenges and dangers to his own life. In both instances we see a man who knew how to be firm in the face of extreme challenge.

When Peter the apostle was addressing the early church leaders he described Paul and Barnabas as leaders who had risked their lives for the gospel. "It seemed good to us, being assembled with one accord, to send chosen men to you with our beloved Barnabas and Paul, men who have risked their lives for the Name of our Lord Jesus Christ (Acts 15:25-26).

These words were spoken in defense of the ministries of Paul and Barnabas in a time of great theological and leadership debate. Peter's emphasis was that Paul and Barnabas qualified to take the message from the Jerusalem council because they had not only been faithful in their service for the Lord, but had also risked their lives while in this noble service. These men lived in constant dangers to their lives as they preached the message of Christ in their day. This aspect of being bold and courageous in times of danger was noted by the other Apostles. They argued that for this reason alone, these two men qualified to represent the church leadership wherever they went.

Paul knew by experience the price that one had to pay in the service of the King. In Second Corinthians, Paul gives a list of the struggles and trials that he had to undergo just to be in the ministry of the gospel. "From the Jews five times I received forty stripes minus one. Three times I was beaten with rods; once I was stoned; three times I was shipwrecked; a night and a day I have been in the deep; in journeys often, in perils of waters, in perils of robbers, in perils of my own countrymen, in perils of the Gentiles, in perils in the city, in perils in the wilderness, in perils in the sea, in perils among false brethren; in weariness and toil, in sleeplessness often, in hunger and thirst, in fastings often, in cold and nakedness (2 Corinthians 11:24-27).

Such a listing and also the situation of facing a whole community who are about to stone you for your faith leave us wondering why any of us would complain for the few trials we go through. I have heard many complains from believers that do not compare at all with the experiences of Joshua and Caleb or even those of Paul. For the last few years I have been living in America and it makes one laugh to hear of some of the things that some people call, "suffering for Christ."

Like Paul, both Joshua and Caleb did not retreat in the face of opposition or trials. Nothing would cause them to turn away from their faith in God. Their minds were set to reaching the land of promise. They were not afraid of the descendants of Anak, the mighty giants who scared the other ten spies. They were not afraid or affected by the negativity and pessimism of the other ten spies. Caleb's response was, "If the Lord delights in us, then He will bring us into this land and give it to us, a land which flows with milk and honey" (Numbers 14:8). These men were faced with life threatening dangers and neither did they change their message nor retreat. Such is the call of God for each and every one of his children. Dr. Joseph Mukuna Nzeketha reminds the church that however bad the situation gets and however bad our communities are, we still have to stand firm for the Lord. "I believe that, no matter how evil the city or community is, it does not force church to abandon its mission or service to these people" (*Is there*, 90). John Hyde, who was better known as, "Praying Hyde," said, "The harder the struggle, the more hope should possess your soul, for Satan only fights hardest where he is more afraid of defeat" (Carre, 160).

A Place of greater Glory

Sometimes I think of Daniel in the lion's den. To everybody else in the city of Babylon, this den full of vicious, hungry lions was the most dangerous and scariest place to be; but not so for Daniel. To him this was the place of greater glory. It was the place where the Lord was about to demonstrate his power over His creation, over Daniel's enemies and also elevate Daniel to the next level. God was about to use the darkness of this valley in Daniel's life to bring even greater glory to Himself than when Daniel was in his own bedroom. It was in this dark pit that Daniel's faithfulness would become a testimony to the nations; and that for many generations in the future.

Because of Daniel's steadfastness and unwavering faith in God, the following day King Darius made a decree that the God of Daniel should be feared and worshipped in the whole of his realm. "To all peoples, nations and languages that dwell in all the earth: Peace be multiplied to you. I make a decree that in every dominion of my kingdom men must tremble and fear before the God of Daniel. For he is the living God, and steadfast forever; His kingdom is the one, which shall not be destroyed, and His dominion shall endure to the end. He delivers and rescues, and He works signs and wonders in heaven and on earth, who has delivered Daniel from the power of the lions" (Daniel 6:25-27).

> God always uses these valley experiences to bring even greater glory to His glorious Name and blessings to His people. He does so when His people choose to take risks for His Name's sake.

Greater Glory from the Valley Experience

God always uses these valley experiences to bring even greater glory to His glorious Name and blessings to His people. He does so when His people choose to take risks for His Name's sake.

Trials and afflictions may sometimes seem like instruments to bring us down, but when we stand firm in times of these hard times, God will always turn them for our good and for the establishment of His kingdom. Such experiences, like in the life of Paul and Barnabas strengthens one's leadership position in lives of those he leads and in the eyes of the other believers. Blackaby says, "A willingness to sacrifice gives leaders more authority with their people than does their position on an organizational chart" (*Spiritual*, 190).

If Caleb had not encountered the challenge and opposition from the other negative spies, we would not have heard of him and neither would the Lord have used him as greatly as He did. His stand in the times of problems promoted him to service of a higher level. God always uses these valley experiences to bring even greater glory to His glorious Name; when we choose to take risks for His Name's sake. This should teach us to stand firm and steadfast when faced with opposition and trials. Do not ever be tempted to give up when things get rough. You never know what the Lord is about to do. It could be that your present valley experience will be the one that the Lord will use to catapult you to the next level. Only be faithful and face the challenge by faith.

Called to life of Courage

Both Joshua and Caleb noticed that the people of Israel had given themselves to the spirit of fear. They were afraid of facing the enemy. This fear paralyzed the very people who had left Egypt with great excitement and expectation after they had seen the hand of God at work. How soon we forget God's working in our midst when faced with new challenges? We forget that He who fought our battles in the past will fight our battles in the present and also in the future. The people of Israel had witnesses the power of God as he overcame the most powerful nation on earth. If God could conquer Egypt, definitely He would conquer any nation on the face of the earth. How fast we forget God's intervention in our lives. If only the Israelites had remembered how the Lord had given them a great and mighty deliverance on the night of the Passover.

Caleb and his friend quieted the people, "Only do not rebel against the Lord nor fear the people of the land, for they are our bread, their protection has departed from them and the Lord is with us. Do not fear them (Numbers 14:9). Any fear, negativity, and pessimism is a hindrance to any service we can render to our heavenly Father. In Caleb's mind, these large giants were already defeated. "They are our bread…their protection has departed from them." Caleb understood God's promises for his people. The size and power of the enemy did not amount to much when the Lord was on their side.

Fear: An Enemy to Faith

Fear and faith cannot be bedfellows. They cannot abide together. A child of God will take chance and face any challenge as long as they know that they are on God's side. Paul the Apostle told his spiritual son Timothy that God has not given us the spirit of fear but of power, of love and of sound mind (2 Timothy 1:7).

When any of us walks in fear, then it becomes hard to serve the Lord effectively. Most of the time fear leads to defeat and frustration. It is more like what Job says, "For *the thing* I greatly *feared has come upon me*. And what I dreaded *has* happened to *me*" (Job 3:25). When we ignore God's word, which tells us to continually and constantly walk in faith and steadfastly trust Him, then we will usually experience the very things we were afraid would happen to us. From our story in the book of Numbers this is exactly what happened. The ten spies feared defeat and death. In the very day they rejected God's word and in their action also rejected His immediate directive, they quickly reaped the fruit of their disobedience, fear, and unbelief (Numbers 14:37). They all died on the very day of their negative confession. Even though the rest of the nation would still die in the wilderness, these ten paid for their stubbornness and unbelief on that very day!

You inherit what you Say

One of the lessons I have learned from these spies is that of not only trusting in God's hand in the midst of life's challenges, but also to watch what I say. Words have power. The scriptures say, "Death and life are in the power of the tongue, and those who love it will eat its fruit" (Proverbs 18:21). The positive words of Caleb that were in agreement with God's word became a reality in his own life and also brought blessing to his future generation. His words were no longer just words, but real tangible and observable experiences. His word had mentioned the defeat of God's enemies and the victory of His people. As a result of Caleb's obedience and confession, God Himself declared that even his future generations would benefit from his life of faith (Numbers 14:24). He inherited exactly what he said, "A land flowing with milk and honey."

Say what He says – God's very Words

This story reminds me of a Greek word, "**homologeo**," which means to "to speak the same thing". In our conversations we need to practice speaking words that agree with what God has already said. This is what caused the lives of Joshua and Caleb to stand out. They simply confessed what God had said and not how they felt or what experience had taught them. As I said in a previous passage, sometimes our experience can become a problem in matters of faith, because at times the Lord will lead you into areas that your experience will say, "I have been there, done that and failed." Those are the times you learn to walk by faith and not by sight.

Good positive confession is good but not enough. God does not necessarily fulfill our personal wishes. The world would be a mess if the Lord would fulfill every wish His children made. There are so many people today making all kinds of confessions and believing that the Lord will become more like their errand boy and accomplish their will. God does not accomplish our will. God will never fulfill our wishful thinking and our worldly aspirations. He fulfills his own will that is established in His word and in His person. That's why sometime we pray for some things for a long time and the prayers go unanswered.

Line up with His will and Purpose

This is the reason why it is very important that we get to know His word and also have constant communion with Him. It is only when we abide in His presence daily and also feast at His table that we will understand His will and purpose for our lives. Our prayers also will begin to line up with His will and purposes. Prayers that are prayed in accordance with God's word will get God's attention.

The scripture admonishes us to delight ourselves in the Lord, and as a result the Lord will fulfill the desires of our heart (Psalm 37:4). People have quoted this verse without taking into consideration the first part of the verse. It is only when we delight ourselves in the Lord–when we seek His will and delight to walk in His ways; when we delight to be and do what the Lord desires, then it becomes an obvious thing that the Lord will honor our desires because those desires will no longer be just our desires but will be His too.

You are Precious

We need to understand this; there is nothing in the whole wide world that is too good, or too precious for a child of God. Jesus affirms this as he taught his disciples. "Are not five sparrows sold for two copper coins? And not one of them is forgotten before God. But the very hairs of your head are all numbered. Do not fear therefore; you are of more value than many sparrows (Luke 12:6-7). Jesus says that you and I are very valuable in the eyes of God. Do not allow the devil or any of his followers to belittle you. You are precious in the eyes of God.

The bible says, "For the Lord God is a sun and shield; The Lord will give grace and glory; No good thing will He withhold from those who walk uprightly (Psalm 84:11). Even in this passage which has been quoted quite often to prove that the Lord will definitely supply our needs and wants; it is very clear what kind of people the Lord will respond to with His blessings; It is to those who will walk in His ways.

Like Caleb, we too, can claim God's blessing. Whatever we ask for has to be for the benefit of God's kingdom, and for the glory of His great Name. When you "name and claim," some things, always ask yourself, "Does what I ask for, bring glory to the Father? Does it make me a more effective witness of the love of God? I like the words of Caleb when he saw the unbelief of the rest of the nation, "If the Lord delights in us, then He will bring us into this land and give it to us, 'a land which flows with milk and honey" (Numbers 14:8).

At this point Caleb's greatest interest was not his comfort, but in what God's will would be, and what would bring pleasure and glory to his heavenly Father. This is a great lesson for each of us. If the Lord delights in your ways as you obey His word, He will release your "Canaan." Some of us have been roaming for many years in the wilderness. All we need to do is practice pleasing the Lord. If the Lord will delight in your ways, He will also release that blessing you've been waiting for. It does not take long for the Lord to release your Canaan's blessings if and when your ways please Him.

Such an attitude should set the standard by which we judge our walk with the Lord and our prayer and devotional lives. "Does what I say, do, or think honor the Lord?" Does it extend God's kingdom either in me or in those around me? If not, then I should not expect the Father to honor my prayers. However, if what I am involved in, and that which I desire is in His will and purpose for my life, God obligates Himself to answer such prayer. "If you abide in me, and my words abide in you, you will ask what you desire, and it shall be done for you" (John 15:7).

Note that the Lord does place a condition to the fulfillment of the promise. "If you abide in Me, and my words abide in you." In other words, if we do not abide in Him, and do not live in accordance to His word, then we should not expect him to respond positively to our prayers. If you are not abiding, then what business do you have making requests to the Father? This may sound negative, but it is His love reaching out to us. He desires intimate fellowship with His children. This divine friendship will also produce the answerability of our prayers.

Our Lord told the disciples, "Do not fear, little flock, for it is your Father's good pleasure to give you the kingdom" (Luke 12:32). You really do not need to persuade the Lord to bless you; for He will indeed bless, as you learn to walk in His will and to practice pleasing Him, by living a life that honors and glorifies Him. He desires to give us the kingdom. That's why Paul would say, "Therefore we make it our aim, whether present or absent, to be well pleasing to Him (2 Corinthians 5:9).

The fact that our heavenly Father demands that we be in tune with His will in our lives should not be viewed negatively as has been viewed by many people. The point here is, we should differentiate the demands of human religious leaders and God's will and purpose for our lives. Sometimes what has been burdensome and frustrating to the church members are not God's requirements, but rather religious requirement based on the traditions of men.

I would like us to note something about Caleb. He only asked or declared those things that were already established by God in His word. God had already promised the land of Canaan to the Patriarchs and also to the nation of Israel. Caleb was not asking anything outside of God's revealed will. He only prayed and made declaration of what God had promised. This is why God answered his prayer and fulfilled all of his desires because each and every one of his desires and declarations was based on God's word. If only we could follow Caleb's example. We could easily have our prayers answered.

Words for Necessary Edification

A few years ago, I lived and worked in an area where lots of people used all kinds of profanity. Actually I was shocked as to how bad the language of some of these people was. Even when not annoyed or in distress, they still used coarse language. I was reminded of the warning given to the believers of the kind of language that we are supposed to use. "Let no corrupt word proceed out of your mouth, but what is good for necessary edification, that it may impart grace to the hearers" (Ephesians 4:29). The apostle James poses a question to the believers, "Does a spring send forth fresh water and bitter from the same opening? (James 3:11). The idea here is that true believers will always seek to speak that which is true and will also watch how they speak, the words they use, and in what occasion or season they speak those words. The Bible says, "A word fitly spoken is like apples of gold in settings of silver (Proverbs 25:11).

I want to illustrate this with a story from one of my family members. Steve, one of my brothers-in-law who was very close to me died in a car accident, and within a year he was followed by his brother Sammy who was a well-known Kenyan Christian comedian, who went by the name, Masaduku Arap Simiti. The news of the passing away of these two precious people was very hard for most of us in the family and especially to their aging parents. Both of these men died in the prime of their lives and had actually talked about serving the Lord closely with me just before each of them died.

When Sammy died, it was quite difficult even to think of words of comfort to give to this precious couple. I remember it very vividly. When I met with the parents the pain and sorrow was so evident. Then one holier than thou lady came to comfort them. She told Baba Masaduku as we fondly call the father, "You need not mourn like this. You should remember the story of Job. Job lost everything including his children and ..." Before she could continue with her "preachy message," Baba Masaduku stopped her in mid-sentence. "I don't need this now. Listen to me! My name is not Job! Do you hear? My name is not job."

What I mean by telling this story is that we need to understand that there are words that may be good, but when spoken in the wrong season, they do not help. If anything such words or even preaching become an aggravation than a blessing. What this woman forgot is that several of those who visited Baba Masaduku's family were better preachers than she, but they still held their peace and allowed the family to mourn the passing away of their beloved son, especially with the understanding that they had just lost another son within eleven months. This is what Paul means when he writes, "Weep with those who weep" (Romans 12:15). There are times to just weep and not preach!

Words Matter

I have an interesting example of how I learned not to use curse, swear words or profanity. Even though I have never been one that used curse words even before I came to know Chris, I still had words that I used that I had picked up from the community I grew up in. Some of us found out after we grew up that some of the words we had picked up as we grew, especially those in the English language were terrible curse words. We did not know how bad and unacceptable these words or phrases were until we grew up and in some cases these words had become part of our vocabulary. We used these words freely without shame or regret. These words had come to our African communities through the colonial masters. Many of our parents and relatives had worked for the colonial masters and picked some of their curse words without any consideration of what these words really meant. I can still remember one very bad curse word that we used very freely as we grew up, only to learn later, when we learned the English language how dirty the word was.

It was thirty-three years ago and I had just come to the USA and enrolled at the Rosedale Bible Institute, in Irwin, Ohio. Since I was just learning how to drive, this actually amused my American friends since I was twenty-six years old. Most

Americans learn how to drive at age sixteen or eighteen. Anyway, one day I had requested one of the young people to drive me to the church where I was going to preach. These great Mennonite young people were always kind and willing to take me to the different churches where I would minister. A few other young people joined us on this trip.

Swear words and Curse Words

On this one occasion we were discussing on something. I cannot remember exactly what the subject matter was, but I can still remember my response especially because of what happened on this day. One of the young people asked me, "Armstrong, if someone did that to you what would you say?" Without even thinking twice I answered, "I would tell them to go to hell!" When I said those words everybody in the car got extremely quiet. I was surprised and wondered what it was that I had said that had shocked my friends to that extent. For some time nobody said a word. Finally, one of the young people gained courage to speak and asked me, "Armstrong, don't you understand that what you just said was a curse word?" I responded, "What is a curse word?"

Up until that day I knew of only three ways the word curse was used. I knew that if we did not obey God and lived lives that dishonored Him, such behavior would lead to God's wrath and judgment. The second way I understood a curse is the negative pronouncement by a parent to a child especially to the children who have been disrespectful to the parents. Many communities in Africa take curses from their parents very seriously, especially the curses that are pronounced just before the death of the parents. The third way I understood this word was in relations to witchcraft and wizardly. I knew that witches and wizards did cast spells and curses on people. I had heard many stories of people who had experienced very negative things because of some spells being cast on them.

By the way, now that I have mentioned something about curses by witches and wizards I need to explain one important thing. Those who have received Jesus Christ as Lord and Savior need not fear the power of witches and wizards. There is no power that can penetrate the blood of Jesus Christ. Like that old chorus that speaks about hiding under the blood, a child of God is totally secure when under the blood of God's own son.

The demons trembled when they heard of Jesus during his earthly ministry (Mark 1:21-27). He has not changed. The Bible says that Jesus Christ is the same, yesterday, today and forever (Hebrews13:8). During His earthly ministry He gave His disciples power to cast out demons. The first disciples went out and preached the gospel and actually cast demons out of people (See Luke 10:17-19). The disciple served the Lord in their day, and now you and I are the instruments that the Lord desires to use to overcome the kingdom of the enemy. He has filled us with the same Spirit that He gave to the early church and He expects his church today to be as effective as the early church in combating the hordes of the kingdom of darkness. The power and authority over demons is still available to the church of Jesus Christ.

> He has filled us with the same Spirit that He gave to the early church and He expects his church today to be as effective as the early Church in combating the hordes of the kingdom of darkness.

To return to my story with those Mennonite Bible School Students - when I thought about it later I came to understand that I knew exactly what these young people were saying, except that in Africa we would have just called it bad words or coarse language. All the same up until that day I had never thought anything about telling people to "go to hell." When I think about it now, I cannot believe that nobody had warned me about this carelessness of speech over all these years. I came to know Christ as Savior at age fourteen in 1970 and began preaching two years later, and yet for these twelve years of ministry nobody had warned me of the use of this particular curse word.

When I think about it now I realize that this is probably the worst curse words that anybody can use, and yet I hear it all the time especially in America. The Americans have even now changed the word "hell" as to hide it's real meaning. Most often you will hear young people saying, "What the heck?" as an exclamatory remark of surprise. As a believer I should watch very carefully what I say. First, how could I who already believes in the doctrine of heaven and hell wish someone "to go to hell?" Isn't this then the worst curse you could wish on your worst enemy? The bible says that God does not wish for any to perish but that everybody would come to repentance (2 Peter 3:9).

If God wishes for all people to come to repentance and thus escape hell how can we wish even one single soul to, "go to Hell." Can you imagine how the enemy of our souls rejoices when he hears the very people who claim to love the Savior wishing people to go to "his Hell?"

Over the years I have trained and disciplined myself to say the right words. I have come to understand both from secular research and from the scriptures that words are not empty. They carry weight and impact those who hear them. As a child of the King of kings I also realize the kind of responsibility I carry. I represent the King as His ambassador. As his representative I understand that my words have divine ability and should not be uttered carelessly.

Jesus told us that those things we bind on earth are bound in heaven and whatever things we loose on earth are loosed in heaven (See Matthew 18:18). Our words, therefore, have imperial power. We can bind and loose just by speaking. I have then to be very careful of the words I speak; because each of the words I speak will influence those who hear them. I want to be kingdom minded even in the words I speak. I want my words to be a blessing and not a curse to those who hear them. Words are not neutral. They carry either a positive or negative influence.

This seems to have been one of the secret of Caleb's success. He not only had the faith to believe God in tough times, but knew also how to utilize his faith in the words he spoke. His words lined up with his faith and also with God's promises. No wonder he had influence and favor with God.

One thing that each of us needs to know is, "It really does not matter how much I name and claim, if my words and declarations do not line up with God's word. If, however, your words line up with God's will as revealed in His Word, you will be surprised at the effect and impact your words will have.

Armstrong Cheggeh

Lessons from Chapter 2

THERE IS NO CHALLENGE that is too risky when God is involved. There is no valley too dark when God's presence abides with us.

I would rather be in God's presence than be in the most comfortable of places or situations. The darkest and coldest of dungeons can be a place of real peace when God's presence is abiding in an individual's life.

Trials and afflictions may sometimes seem like instruments to bring us down, but when we stand firm in times of challenge, God will always turn them for our good and for the establishment of His kingdom.

Do not ever be tempted to give up when things get rough. You never know what the Lord is about to do. It could be that your present valley experience will be the one that the Lord will use to catapult you to the next level. Only be faithful and face the challenge by faith.

Any fear, negativity, and pessimism are a hindrance to any service we can render to our heavenly Father.

When we ignore God's word, which tells us to continually and constantly walk in faith and steadfastly trust Him, then we will usually experience the very things we were afraid would happen to us.

God will never fulfill our wishful thinking and our worldly aspirations. He fulfills his own will that is established in His word and in His person.

We need to understand this; there is nothing in the whole world that is too good or too precious for a child of God.

Jesus says that you and I are very valuable in the eyes of God. Do not allow the devil or any of his followers to belittle you. You are precious in the eyes of God.

When you "name and claim," some things, always ask yourself, "Does what I ask for bring glory to the Father? Does it make me a more effective witness of the love of God?

We should differentiate between the demands of human religious leaders and God's will and purpose for our lives. Sometimes what has been burdensome and frustrating to the church members are not God's requirements, but rather religious requirement based on the traditions of men.

Those who have received Jesus Christ as Lord and Savior need not fear the power of witches and wizards. There is no power that can penetrate the blood of Jesus Christ.

I have come to understand both from secular research and from the scriptures that words are not empty. They carry weight and impact those who hear them.

Chapter 3

Fear is a Snare

> *"The fear of man brings a snare, But whoever trusts in the Lord shall be safe"* (Proverbs 29:25).

YOU'LL REMEMBER THAT the main sin that hindered the ten spies from accomplishing God's will and purpose both for themselves as well as for the nation of Israel was the sin of fear and not trusting in God's promises. When people give themselves to the spirit of fear, they cannot experience all that God has for them. When we allow fear into our lives, then we cannot experience God's power and anointing in our lives.

Usually when people encounter a situation that would bring extreme fear, they respond in several ways. Some people respond in ways that honor the Lord, while others respond in ways that dishonor our heavenly Father. Ten of the Israelite leaders who went to spy out the land of Canaan with Caleb saw the very things that both Joshua and Caleb saw. They experienced the very things that these two men of God experienced but their responses were so negative that it aggravated the Lord and brought great calamity not only for the ten spies but also for the whole nation of Israel except for Joshua and Caleb.

When faced with great challenges or fear in our lives, we usually respond in any of these three ways: the flight mode, the attack mode and the freeze mode.

The Flight Mode

First we may be caught in the flight mode. This is where we quickly try to avoid the thing or situation that contributed to our fear.

Let me tell you a real life story that happened to me to illustrate this. About eighteen years ago I decided to give my wife a surprise gift for her birthday. I told her to set apart several days before and after her birthday, so we could do something special together, but our destination was to be a surprise. I instructed her to pack casual clothes and a couple of dressy outfits.

When the day finally arrived, we left Nairobi early for the surprise destination. I had told a friend of mine to book me a room at a nice Safari hotel. He chose the Sarova hotel in the Maasai Mara Game reserve. Both my wife and I had never visited this wildlife sanctuary and had always longed to do so. I have always felt bad that even though these beautiful, exotic animal reservations are right in our own country very few citizens ever visit them. It has always been a privilege enjoyed only by a few wealthy Africans and foreign tourist. I had always wanted to visit these places and today was the day. I was so excited to share this special experience with my wife.

When we got to the town of Narok we stopped for lunch and also to visit with some of my relatives, Bishop Sammy and Alice Muriu who own and operate the Kim Dishes restaurant. We had a wonderful time of fellowship and visited much longer than we had planned. We did not realize that the distance remaining was almost as much as we had covered. We left Narok in late afternoon and headed for Maasai Mara.

For some reason we did not see the signs that would let us know that we had arrived in the "animal kingdom." We got lost and followed a much longer route. To make matters worse, we hit a bolder on the road and my exhaust system broke down! The car started making a lot of noise. After sometime, without realizing that we were right in the most dangerous part of the park, I stopped the vehicle and got out to examine the exhaust system. I realized that there wasn't much I could do and decided to continue until we got to our destination where we could get help.

I had started the car and we had only gone a distance of less than a quarter of a kilometer when a large lion jumped from the bushes on the side of the road right in our pathway! Apparently the lion had not heard the noise from our car until it got in front of us. As soon as the lion heard the loud noise coming toward it, it quickly jumped out of the way! Of course we also took off very fast! Both my wife and I were really shaken, especially because I had just been out of the car. We did not even want to think of what might have happened if I had tools and had tried to fix the problem with the exhaust system.

I am telling you this story not only to let you know of God's goodness in protecting His people from danger, but also to make a point about fear. When the lion, which is supposed to be bravest of all animals, heard the loud noise, it did not stand there to see what would happen. It jumped out of the way. Even the brave lions have a sense of fear. What the lion did is what we also do sometimes when faced with fear. It is the flight mode. We run away from whatever it is that threatens us.

> *In the real life situations there are definite times when we can flee from some situation. God has placed this instinct in us for our good.*

In the real life situations there are definite times when we can flee from some situation. God has placed this instinct in us for our good. In the Bible there is a story where Jacob, one of the patriarchs of the nations of Israel, had to flee for his life and the lives of his family. His sons, Simeon and Levi, had secretly hatched a plan to punish the Hivites for defiling their sister Dinah (Genesis 34:1-2). They tricked the Hivites to receive circumcision with the promise that now they could allow them to marry their sister. The sons of Jacob came in the night, while the Hivite men were sore, and in pain, and killed them all.

Jacob was very angry about his sons' action, and even many years later, on his death-bed remembered this cruel act as he spoke his final farewell and blessing to his sons (Genesis 49:5-7). However, even with his anger, there is one thing he did not do. He did not wait to see what would happen now that his sons had murdered all the men of the Hivite clan. He knew that the neighboring Canaanite tribes might gather together and attack his family. He therefore moved his family hastily from that place to another place. Fear was the motivation that got him out of that place hastily.

Like Jacob, there are times when some situations can cause us to flee and go to some other place. However, each of us needs to be careful that we flee, not just for comfort sake, but only if our security and safety would be to the glory of God. I need to explain this a little. There are times that the Lord may call us into situations of danger, not because He is a sadistic God, but because He is able to see the end from the beginning (Isaiah 46:10). Our God is not limited by time and space. He knows that some of the seemingly bad situations will eventually bring greater honor than the good or comfortable situations would. He, therefore, may at times call you into such situations so that eventually, all things turn out for your own good, since you are his child and called according to His divine purposes (See Romans 8:28). Our brother, Lloyd-Jones, observes; "Yet it is a fundamental principle in life and walk of faith that we must always be prepared for the unexpected when we are dealing with God" (*Faith, Tried*, 11).

> Our God is not limited by time and space. He knows that some of the seemingly bad situations will eventually bring greater honor than the good or comfortable situation would.

Sometimes our fear is based on some painful or negative experiences we have had in the past. We tend to avoid the experience and like the lion in our story, we get into a flight mode. We run away from the source of fear hoping that we will escape the pain we experienced in the past. That again may sound like a good reason to flee or avoid the negative experiences. We need to always remember that the best place to be is in the will of God, however dangerous the place or experience is. There may be times that the best place that also honors the Lord is the "danger zone." We, however, need to watch out that we do not place our lives in danger just to prove that we are bold in our faith.

Caleb challenged the nations of Israel to believe God and move forward to possess the land of promise. "Let us go up at once and take possession, for we are well able to overcome it" (Numbers 13:30). Caleb, of all people, knew the dangers ahead. He had personally seen the sons of Anak, who were also mighty giants, but he trusted in God's power to give victory to His people. Our boldness as we face life's challenges should not be founded on what we can do on our own, but rather on what the Lord can do with us or for us. That's why our brother Paul can declare, "I can do all things through Christ who strengthens me" (Philippians 4:13).

The Freeze Mode

The other way we respond in times of fear is freezing – being completely immobile and leaving the enemy or whatever the source of fear was to do whatever it planned in one's life. Let me illustrate this with another true wildlife story. After going on the first Safari to the game reservations, I liked it so much that I have visited several parks after that first trip to Maasai Mara. A year or so later my wife and I were accompanied by some friends for a much needed vacation to the Amboseli National Park. From this park you enjoy the beautiful sights of Mount Kilimanjaro and the famous Amboseli elephants.

While in the Amboseli Serena we met one of the hotel tour guides who told us about an incident which had just occurred. An American tour group was staying at the hotel and the tour guide told them of a boa constrictor which had just swallowed a whole antelope. He explained to them that when the boa constrictor has swallowed up a large animal it is usually immobile and is not a threat to anybody while in that state until the animal it has swallowed is digested and the snake can now move freely. Actually it is very easy to kill this snake while it is in this state.

When the American team heard this story they were more than excited! This is the kind of story they had only heard and seen on Television. Today was the day to see the real thing. They requested the tour guide to take them to the place where the snake lay. As they walked they were so excited and making a lot of noise. Then just in front of them they saw a large brownish bolder. No, it was not a large stone. It was the Boa constrictor! The tour guide pointed at the snake and told them "this is the snake." Everybody stopped and the place got real quiet. Everybody was shocked! They knew it would be a big snake but not this big!

For a while nobody uttered a word. Then one of the American ladies in the team just froze! She could not move. She stood there paralyzed by fear. Then she pointed her finger at her husband and said, "I knew it. I just knew it. You brought me to Africa to feed me to the snakes!" She was shocked and completely out of herself. She was illogical and disoriented. They had to carry her back to the hotel!

This illustrates the other reaction to fear. There are some things that come our way and shock us to an extent that we freeze and are not able to face life realistically. There are circumstances that sometimes come our way and render us completely immobile, physically or emotionally. Sometimes that's how people get mental break downs. Something comes into their lives that make them "freeze" in the mind.

Let's examine this aspect of extreme fear for a moment. All of us will face times of challenge. Sometimes these challenges are so threatening that we tend to be overwhelmed. I know I have personally faced such challenges. I will never forget when such a thing happened to me. There was a season in my life when I was experiencing great success in the ministry and was really excited about what the Lord was doing in my own life, in my family and in the local church. I couldn't ask for more. Something drastic happened that changed the course of my ministry permanently. To be brief, a conspiracy was hatched to bring me down as a leader in this one organization. Even though I had known for a long time that there were negative feelings toward me from certain leaders, I did not let it bother me. I had always believed that if I did my work well, I would always be safe to continue serving the Lord without interruption in this particular organization. I was wrong and learned the hard way.

When the leadership met it was determined even before the meeting began and even before I got there that I would be forced to leave the organization and they must fabricate a story about me. To make the story short, this group succeeded so well in their plans. I left the meeting devastated, not so much because I would leave the organization, but because of the conspiracy. How could top Christian leaders do this? I was shocked! I guess that is why the Bible says, "Cursed is the man that trusts in man" (Jeremiah 17:5).

I had trusted this group of people to the extent that when they hatched this conspiracy about me, I found it extremely hard to accept what had just transpired. I went home and literally fell apart! For the next several days I could barely do anything. I stayed mostly in bed. I would lie down quietly for long periods of time so that my wife would come to the room and touch me just be make sure I was alive. When I opened my mouth to speak the only questions I asked over and over was, "How could they do this?" Can Christian leaders do this?" I guess my trust in man was so deep that it almost cost me my mind! No wonder the Bible admonishes us to trust in the Lord with all our hearts and not lean upon our own understanding (Proverbs 3:5). The emphasis here is the need to trust fully in God and not in man.

There are circumstances that sometimes come our way and render us completely immobile, physically or emotionally.

What gave me life and strength even in this season of the valley was my deep trust in God. I was not only sure of God's call upon my life, but I had experienced His power and grace many times and on many occasions. I had learned to trust in the Lord in difficult times. Even though I had trusted men to some level, my trust in the Hand of God was still very firm. I could still trust Him to see me through the difficult times in my life. The valley experiences in my past made me know that this too would pass. I spent lots of hours praying. I knew that I could not handle this by myself and that I needed His hand. I cried to Him and the Holy Spirit comforted me in a most amazing way.

When faced with these real deep valley experiences, which would tempt any of us to give up, we should be reminded that the Lord who has seen us through in times, past will come to our rescue. He is ever faithful. He does not leave us at the mercy of our enemies. His rod and staff comfort us even in the valley of the shadow of death (Psalm 23:4). The Scriptures tell us to call upon Him in the day of trouble and that He shall rescue us (Psalms 50:15). I experienced that deliverance during that time of trials.

Another aspect that gave me strength in this time of need is my family. The Bible says that he that finds a good wife finds a good thing (Proverbs 18:22). My wife is such a wonderful gift from the Lord. She has stood by me, "for better and for worse." She is indeed a Proverbs 31 kind of woman. During that time of great trials, she stood with me and encouraged me. She would come into the room and remind me of God's goodness to us. "Don't let this thing worry you. God will see us though." She would then pray with me and remain with me for long periods of time.

For those of you who are married, please learn to value your spouse. Not only so that they can be of help in times of need, but because it is the right thing to do and because it honors our heavenly Father. When you invest in loving, caring, and supporting your spouse, when the times of challenge come, the spouse becomes a valuable and helpful support in return.

Good and godly friends are also very important when it comes to seasons of challenge. Any time I have experienced a hard time, I have found great comfort in having friends I can turn to for strength. In my first book, *Developing Relationships with Integrity*, I emphasized the need to have what I called "covenant prayer partners" (144). These are a few friends that you get to know closely and to whom you can open your heart to, from time to time. They are people you can call at any time of the night when you are in need and they would not complain. Each of us needs such friends.

If you do not have three to five of such friends, you will need to pray that the Lord will give you such friends, but be reminded of what the Bible says about friendships. "A man who desires to have friends must show himself friendly (Proverbs 18:24). You cannot expect to have such committed and faithful friends if you do not become such a person yourself. Friendships need cultivation. The more you open up to someone and talk to them often, the closer your relationship will become. Boniface Gitau advises Christian leaders to make sure that they develop such relationships as they continue serving the Lord. "Wise leaders always choose godly men to advise them and to pray with them. Find the godly people around you who made right choices when they faced the challenges you are now facing. Learn from them" (*Making*, 76). I will discuss friendship more in depth in Chapter 6 of this book.

> *Don't allow yourself to remain alone. Take a step and begin developing closer relationships with the brothers and sisters around where you live.*

When I was hurting so bad, these close friends came to me and supported me. I knew that I was not alone. I had friends standing with me. This has been my experience when going through the storms of life. Don't allow yourself to remain alone. Take a step and begin developing closer relationships with the brothers and sisters around where you live. These people will surround you when you get into "fearful" situations or during times when you feel overwhelmed. My good friend, Dr. Geoffrey Njuguna, reminds the believers and especially those in leadership to learn the value of such close relationships. "We replenish our emotional tanks though meaningful relationships with our family members and other close friends (*Become*, 32). In his book, Nick

Cuthbert reminds the Christian leaders that they were never meant to operate alone. "The gift of leadership may be given to an individual but it was never intended to function in isolation. ... you both offload the weight of responsibility on to each other and it makes the whole load feel lighter" (*How to survive*, 127).

The Attack Mode

The other way we face fear or fearful situations is what is called the "attack mode." We face the enemy or whatever is confronting us head on! It is where you face challenges with a David-like attitude, "The Lord is my light and my salvation, whom shall I fear? The Lord is the strength of my life, of whom shall I be afraid?" (Psalms 27:1).

You face life with the understanding that nothing is greater than our heavenly Father. Whatever enemy comes our way has already been defeated because greater is He who is in us than he who is in the world (1 John 4:4). Whatever battles come our way, we will always come out as conquerors. This is one way our loving heavenly Father trains his children. "Leaders must have the kind of maturity that comes from fighting battles and carrying burdens, maturity that is painfully developed in the school of life" (Wiersbe, 12).

When we look into the Scriptures and especially in the life of Caleb and many other heroes of the faith, we realize that God did not insulate them from fearful experiences or situations that could produce fear. He allowed them to go through these experiences in order that they may learn to trust in Him and not in their own strength. "History is replete with examples of leaders who enjoyed success only after enduring great suffering. Life offers few shortcuts to greatness" (Blackaby, 190).

On numerous occasions you will find the Lord admonishing even the greatest of these heroes not to fear. He told Joshua, "Have I not commanded you? Be strong and of good courage; do not be afraid, nor be dismayed, for the Lord your God is with you wherever you go" (Joshua 1:9). He told Jeremiah, "Do not be afraid of their faces, for I am with you to deliver you," says the Lord" (Jeremiah 1:8).

The fact that the Lord tells us to not fear means that He knows that if left to ourselves we tend to relent to the spirit of fear. Just as discussed earlier, these fears can lead us into situations where we either run away from our calling and duty or we freeze as though inviting the enemy to come and devastate us.

Usually these responses happen when someone has failed in some aspect of their lives. Such people give themselves to the fear of man. They fear what others will say or do about their failures. They hide and avoid those who may be familiar with them. It could be that as you read this book you are hiding or avoiding other believers for fear of rejection or exposure.

Whatever is happening in your life that is causing you to walk in fear can be overcome by trusting in God's mercy and grace. None of us is good. Our own righteousness is like filthy rags (Isaiah 64:6). There is none righteous, no, not one (Romans 3:10). What keeps us walking and serving the King of Kings is His marvelous grace. That popular hymn Amazing Grace, sums it all, "T'was grace that brought me safe thus far, and grace will lead me home." There is no time in our lives that we will not need His amazing grace.

In Psalms 23, the Lord does not promise to remove the valley of the shadow of death. He promises to provide the protection of His rod and staff, while going through the valley of the shadow of death. He will be with us in our valley experiences. The Lord does not promise to remove the valley experiences but rather promises His abiding presence even in the deepest and darkest of valleys. He will never leave us nor forsake us (Hebrews 13:5). I like the words in Isaiah 43:2 "When you pass through the waters, I will be with you; and through the rivers they shall not overflow you. When you walk through the fire, you shall not be burned, nor shall the flame scorch you."

The floods will come, and the fires will burn, but the Lord will be with us in all these situations. He will be the fourth man in the fiery furnace (Daniel 3:25).

Caleb knew God in an intimate way and trusted him during the worst storms in his life. We find that he did not argue with his friends about the size of the giants nor of how fearsome they looked. He did not doubt the size of their cities and how fortified they were. He did not doubt the existence of the enemies since he had seen them with his own eyes, but he dared to doubt their power against the forces of light. He could declare with Paul, "If God be for us who can be against us" (Romans 8:31).

Serving in Obscurity

I just wonder how many of us would continue serving if nobody gave us any form of recognition. How many of us would continue serving without the formal acknowledgment of our person and or ministry?

Some people's confidence, continuity and joy in leadership rely on titles, positions and other human institutional accolades. To many people the ministry has come to mean competition, comparisons, and generally a forum to establish their little personal kingdoms. It was not so for Caleb. For over forty-five years we barely hear of him. Apparently he was not a passive onlooker because after the forty-five years we realize that he was still a recognized leader in the tribe of Judah (Joshua 14: 6-7). We do not know what he did for forty-five years. All we know is that he faithfully served the nation of Israel on a less recognized position than that of Joshua for those forty-five years and all this time remained faithful. He was satisfied to "play the second fiddle" under Joshua for such a long time. Mike Bonem says this of the second fiddle leader, "Second chair leaders intentionally seek to shape the organization's direction and mesh their individual dreams with the broader vision" (*Leading*, 5). Such was Caleb for over forty-five years. He knew, understood, and accepted that the top chair belonged to Joshua, and he served faithfully for forty-five years without jealousy or competition.

Another aspect of Caleb's life is that even after serving

faithfully for forty-five years, he still had not received his inheritance, and yet waited patiently for God's time. It is interesting how some of us serve the Lord for five to ten years and complain a lot that the Lord has not fulfilled His promises to us. Probably we have not waited long enough. Caleb waited for forty-vive years before he got the territory of Hebron (Joshua 14:13-14). Abraham waited twenty-five years for the birth of his son Isaac. The Bible says that, "He did not waver at the promise of God through unbelief, but was strengthened in faith; giving glory to God and being fully convinced that what He had promised He was also able to perform." (Romans 4:20-21).

Moses fled Egypt at age forty and then God prepared him for another forty years while he served as a shepherd in the Median back woods. He was eighty years old when finally the Lord commissioned him to go and lead Israel out of bondage.

Others in the Bible waited for long periods of time before God's promises to them were fulfilled. David was only a lad when the prophet Samuel anointed him to be the leader of God's people. It took many years before he ascended the throne (2 Samuel 2:4), and even then he had to wait another seven years before the whole nation would recognize him as king (2 Samuel 5:3).

> *It is interesting how some of us serve the Lord for five to ten years and complain a lot that the Lord has not fulfilled His promises to us. Probably we have not waited long enough.*

All these men waited patiently for God's time. They all served God in obscurity. They did not receive human recognition for long periods of time and yet continued serving God faithfully. Many times God does not rush with the great men and women that He uses to do great exploits for the kingdom. He seems to always allow for long periods of time for growth and development of character. However, on the human level, when we wait for long periods of time, we tend to think that God has forgotten His promise to us. Sometimes we even try to help the Lord in fulfilling the promises!

Even though I've used the example of Abraham as one who trusted in God to fulfill His promises to him, he also failed in trying to assist the Lord in the fulfillment of His promises. He did not doubt that the Lord would fulfill his promise, but rather felt that the Lord needed his help in making them come to fruition.

Sometimes we have laughed at Abraham's idea of assisting God in His fulfillment of promises, but we often fall into the same mistake. We try to help the Lord by utilizing worldly methodologies to try and fulfill God's promises to us. We need to be reminded that God is faithful and will be true to His word. He will always come through for His children.

Those who know and understand their calling in Christ will keep serving whatever the feelings or whatever the cost. Calvin Miller says, "We keep on serving the call, even when we wonder if our partnership with God has been cancelled. As we go on being faithful, we find that the call sooner or later wakes our sleeping adoration to high confidence once again" (*Into the Depths*, 140).

God's approval should be our Focus

When you serve the Lord, His approval, and His alone, should be your focus. Eventually other people may recognize your work, and sometimes they may never acknowledge or appreciate your ministry. That should not discourage you as long as you know whose servant you are. You may have to serve Him in obscurity for a long time. As long as you are faithful to God's Word and His call upon your life you should never let obscurity and the lack of human recognition discourage you. Keep on serving until the final, "Well done, thou good and faithful servant."

Many people appreciate the great, fruitful, and almost faultless ministry of Dr. Billy Graham. Mention his name anywhere on the face of the earth and people will recognize him as the great preacher of the gospel. Billy Graham's ministry would not have been what it is if he did not have people who have served faithfully behind the curtains. Two of these men come to mind. These two men have served as "second fiddle" to Dr. Billy Graham for over fifty years. These two men are the late George Beverly Shea and Cliff Barrows. They stood by Dr. Billy Graham for many years and served to the best of their abilities, and yet all the time under the shadow of their better known, better recognized friend, Billy Graham.

We should realize that not all of us are called to a "Joshua–level" of ministry. There are just a few top places in any ministry or organization. God calls many of us to serve under other leaders. How many of us can serve faithfully like Caleb who served God without much recognition for forty-five years? There are not many Joshua–level ministries, but there are countless Caleb–level ministries.

Waiting upon the Lord

As you serve the Lord, know that the promise may delay, but always remember this, "A delay is not necessarily a denial." The Bible says, "The Lord is not slack concerning His promises, as some count slackness, but is longsuffering toward us, not willing that any should perish but that all should come to repentance" (2 Peter 3:9). If you have not received that which the Lord has promised, please do not give up. Jesus told us to, "ask, seek, and knock" (Matthew 7:7-10). In the Original Greek bible, the wording is more like, "keep on asking," "keep on seeking," and "keep on knocking."

> As you serve the Lord, know that the promise may delay, but always remember this, "A delay is not necessarily a denial."

Jesus gave the story of the woman who persistently kept on coming to the same judge and for a long time she did not get help from him. Due to her persistence he finally responded to her pleas (Luke 18:2-8). Jesus concluded the story by saying, "And shall God not avenge His own elect who cry out day and night to Him, though He bears long with them?" Jesus was teaching us not to give up even when we've been praying for such a long time and the Lord seems not to be responding to our prayers. However rough the storms, however steep the mountain, however dark the night, we need to keep pressing on. God will definitely come to our rescue, but only in His own time.

Lessons from Chapter 3

WHEN PEOPLE GIVE themselves to the spirit of fear, they cannot experience all that God has for them. When we allow fear into our lives, we cannot experience God's power and anointing.

In real life situations there are definite times when we can flee from some situation. God has placed this instinct in us for our good.

There are times that the Lord may call us into situations of danger, not because He is a sadistic God but because He is able to see the end from the beginning (Isaiah 46:10).

We need to always remember that the best place to be is in the will of God, however dangerous the place or experience is. There may be times that the best place that also honors the Lord is the "danger zone."

Our boldness as we face life's challenges should not be founded on what we can do on our own, but rather on what the Lord can do with us or for us.

As you invest in loving, caring, and supporting your spouse, when the times of challenge come, the spouse becomes such valuable and helpful support in return.

Good and godly friends are also very important when it comes to seasons of challenge.

You cannot expect to have such committed and faithful friends if you do not become such a person yourself. Friendships need cultivation. The more often you open up to someone and talk to them, the closer your relationship will become.

God does not insulate His people from fearful experiences or situations that could produce fear. He allows them to go through these experiences in order to learn to trust in Him and not in their own strength.

The fact that the Lord tells us not to fear means that He knows that if left to and by ourselves we tend to give in to the spirit of fear.

The Lord does not promise to remove the valley experiences but rather promises His abiding presence even in the deepest and darkest of valleys.

Many times God does not rush with the great men and women that He uses to do great exploits for the kingdom. He seems to always allow for long periods of time for growth and development of character.

As long as you are faithful to God's word and His call upon your life you should never let obscurity and the lack of human recognition discourage you. Keep on serving until the final, "Well done thou good and faithful servant.

There are not many Joshua–level ministries, but there are countless Caleb–level ministries.

However rough the storms, however steep the mountain, however dark the night, we need to keep pressing on. God will definitely come to our rescue, but only in his own time.

Chapter 4

Standing Firm In Times Of Opposition

WHEN THE TEN Israelite spies gave a negative report to the children of Israel, their report planted the seeds of unbelief and consequent rebellion in the hearts and minds of the nation (Numbers 14:5-6).

The nation of Israel listened to the negative report and ignored the positive report from Joshua and Caleb. It was bad enough that they rejected the word from these two godly men, but even worse they talked of stoning them to death (Numbers 14:5-10). The position of these two men almost cost them their very lives, but they stood firm on God's truth.

If you have been opposed and attacked for standing for the truth, please understand that you are not alone and neither are you the first to be opposed and ostracized for the sake of truth. Actually the bible states clearly that is you choose godliness, you shall definitely be opposed. "Yes, and all who desire to live godly in Christ Jesus will suffer persecution" (2 Timothy 3:12). True believers have been opposed all through the history of the church and even into the Old Testament times, as we can see in the story of Caleb.

Our Lord himself said that His followers will be opposed while in the world, but promised His peace "I have told you these things, so that in me you may have peace. In this world you will have trouble. But take heart! I have overcome the world." (John

16:33). The idea here is that since our Lord overcame the trials in this world, so shall all His followers who follow him whole-heartedly. He even promised to give us the wisdom and the words to say when we find ourselves in situations of oppositions and persecutions. "But when they arrest you, do not worry about what to say or how to say it. At that time you will be given what to say" (Matthew 10:19).

Whatever is not of Faith is Sin

Another thing we note in this story is that the truth was in the hands of the minority. Joshua and Caleb stood for the truth, while the other ten chose the lie. In this case the lie does not necessarily mean that all that the other spies spoke were lies. We consider them lies in that they questioned God's word, His promises and His power to lead and deliver His people. The scriptures says, "whatever is not from faith is sin" (Romans 14:23). Some of the things that the other spies said were true, but unfortunately were not mixed with faith. They had everything else except the faith element. The scriptures say, "Without faith it is impossible to please God" (Hebrews 11:6).

Most of what these spies said was true. They all agreed that the land was good and that those who lived in the land were of great stature. They all agreed that the cities were walled and impregnable. What they did not agree on was God's word and his promises and His will for His people. Both Joshua and Caleb chose to believe that God was able to do what he promised to His people.

Both Caleb and Joshua knew and believed that the enemy soldiers were of larger statures than that of the Israelite soldiers. They also knew of the greatness and strength of the Canaanite cities but they also believed that nothing in the enemy's camp, however, powerful and mighty could compare or come anywhere close to the glorious power of the almighty God. These two faithful warriors understood that nothing in all of creation would hinder them from fulfilling God's purpose for them and the nation of Israel.

As you face life's battles and the trials that come your way; always remember that the God is on your side (Romans 8:31). ***"El-Elohe-Israel,"*** the God of Israel has never lost a battle, and is not about to lose one. Hold on to His everlasting arms and you will always have the victory. He will set a table before you in the presence of your enemies (Psalms 23:4-5).

God has not left you to do things by yourself. He knows exactly what you are going through and has promised to be with us to the end of this age. He will never leave you nor forsake you (Hebrews 13:5). Keep on holding on to His truth. He will see you through. The battles may rage for some time, but know this, "Your heavenly Father knows exactly what you can take." The scriptures says, "No temptation has overtaken you but such as is common to man" (1 Corinthians 10:13). Our loving heavenly Father will not allow you to face a battle or temptation that is bigger or stronger than you. He loves you so much that He will never allow the enemy to bring temptations that are beyond your power and ability. Paul reminds that we will always be not just conquerors, but more than conquerors (Romans 8:37-39).

Not by human Wisdom

Sometime rationalization may sound as the truth. The case presented by the ten spies was very compelling. Their argument was that since the sons of Anak were big in stature, then their size would mean the enemy's victory. They forgot one very important fact. The God of Israel had promised to give them the land of Canaan and that His power and ability as stated above were no match for any of the gods of Canaan.

According to historical and archaeological data, the walls of Jericho as well as the walls of other cities of the time were wide enough for a modern car to be driven on them! Actually some of the people's houses were built right into the wall. (Smith, *Smith's*, 290-291). Rahab the prostitute lived in such a house (Joshua 2:15).

When the ten spies talked of fortified cities, humanly speaking they were right. These cities seemed impenetrable. God had not told them to go and do it by themselves. He did not even explain how He was going to do it. He just gave them a command. There are times that God may ask you to do something that does not seem to make sense at the time. You are left with the choice of either ignoring the command because it does not seem to make sense or just obeying it and leaving the results to the Lord. The good thing is that our God is a good God and will never mislead you.

Even when it seems that what He has asked you does not make sense, just go on and do it. The Lord says, "For My thoughts are not your thoughts, nor are your ways My ways, says the Lord. For as the heavens are higher than the earth, so are My ways higher than your ways, and my thoughts than your thought" (Isaiah 55:8-9).

Knowing that His ways are higher than mine makes me trust in His wisdom and whatever He commands I simply obey. Apostle James talks of human wisdom. He describes it as, "worldly, fleshly and of the devil" (James 3:15-18). Such was the wisdom of the ten spies. Humanly speaking, their words and arguments made sense and that is why they were able to persuade the nation of Israel.

> What those ten spies forgot and what we too often forget is that God is not limited to human rules, arguments and even logic.

What those ten spies forgot and what we too often forget is that God is not limited to human rules, arguments and even logic. Actually the Lord makes very clear in His word, as quoted above that our thoughts are not His thoughts. What God has decreed to do, no one can stop Him. His promise to the Patriarchs was that He would give their descendants the land of Canaan. No giants, no devils, nothing would hinder or stop God from fulfilling this promises.

You may be reading this book and because of some oppositions or negative forces, you feel like giving up. Listen! If

God has promised, do not let anything discourage you. I urge you to keep on waiting upon Him. He is never late. At the fullness of time He will come. Only be faithful and keep on waiting and trusting in His grace. Your day is at hand. The Lord is about to bring it to pass. Do not let the environment or the economic situations of the times discourage you. The Lord's promises will not be determined by the environment or by the economic situation in the country.

Caleb understood God's ways when he said, "If the Lord delights in us, then He will bring us into this land and give it to us, a land which flows with milk and honey" (Numbers 14:8). In Caleb's mind, nothing could hinder the purposes of God. Hardness of heart, disobedience, and rebellion were the only hindrance to their victory and blessing. Even to this day, these are the only enemies to your faith. Do not allow fear, doubt, and unbelief keep you from the blessings and breakthroughs that the Lord has for you.

In the Wilderness for Too Long

I would like to mention something that is really critical as concerns this story. The nation of Israel would not only have arrived but settled in the land of promise in about two weeks, if the Lord had chosen to lead them directly into the land of Canaan or if they had not rebelled against the Lord and against the leaders that the Lord had placed over them. Instead of two weeks, it took them forty years!

How tragic that a nation that was just a short distance from their destination would be deprived of this rich heritage by the spirit of fear, unbelief and rebellion, and wander in the wilderness for forty years. Isn't this a great lesson and challenge for those of us living in the New Testament dispensation? Paul the apostle says that these things happened to these Old Testament believers to remind us not to be like them in their unbelief and rebellion (1 Corinthians 10:11).

Unfortunately, just like the ancient Israelites some of us are wandering in the wilderness of unbelief, fear, and hopelessness. We forget that Jesus came that we may have life and have it abundantly (John 10:10). Indeed, it is God's will that we live life in its fullness. Our brother Peter reminds that the Lord has already provided us with all that we need for us to live victorious Christian lives. "His divine power has given us everything we need for life and godliness through our knowledge of him who called us by his own glory and goodness" (2 Peter 1:3). However, it is impossible to experience the abundant life when we allow the spirit of fear, doubts, and unbelief to reign in our spirits. "For God has not given us the spirit of fear, but of power, love, and a sound mind (2 Timothy 1:7).

Examine your heart deeply and ask yourself whether there are some aspects of "your Canaan" that you are not experiencing because of fear, doubt, and unbelief. Could it be that some of aspects of the blessing of God are taking 40 years in your life instead of two weeks?

In the 1980s we used to sing a song that said, "Wasted years, wasted years oh how foolish..." I just wonder how many years each of us has wasted? How long will some us remain around these mountains when the Lord wants us to continue with our pilgrimage? One time the Israelites remained around a certain mountain for too long, until the Lord reminded them that it was time to continue with their journey (Deuteronomy 2:3). There are times we tend to remain in a particular place for too long. We need to walk closely to the father so that we can be sensitively to the plodding of his Spirit. We do not need to move too fast, and neither do we want to stay in one place for too long.

Godly Sorrow

When the nation of Israel decided to rebel against God and his anointed leaders, both Joshua and Caleb as well as Moses and Aaron tore their clothes and fell on their faces in intercession for the people of God. It is interesting to note that they were not as much concerned about their safety and comfort as they were of

God's honor. They did not worry that they would lose their lives, families and wealth. They did not even care about their names and reputation.

Their sorrow was for the sake of God's name and also for the nation of Israel. God's name and reputations was their greatest concern. These leaders were not sorrowful for themselves, although they were in danger of being stoned to death. Their sorrow and anguish of the soul were not based on the conviction of sin on their own part, but more for the sins of the nation of Israel.

The Lord was angry with the nation of Israel, especially when they suggested that they get a new leader other than God's appointed leader to lead them back to Egypt. He threatened to destroy that generation and make a new one for Moses to lead. It was only after the intercession of the men of God that the Lord spared the nation of Israel.

What becomes your greatest concern when things are not going on well in your home or ministry?

It is important that we note these godly leaders did not campaign for their acceptance or their positions of leadership. They did not even plead for their lives. They campaigned for God's glory. What the nation of Israel did with positions of leadership was not of prime importance in the minds of Moses and these other godly leaders. What mattered most was God's honor and glory.

What becomes your greatest concern when things are not going on well in your home or ministry? Our greatest concern, most of the time, is our wellbeing, our provision and our personal or family security. Jesus taught us that these things ought not to be our greatest concern. "Therefore, I say to you, do not worry about your life, what you will eat or what you will drink; nor about your body, what you will put on, is not life more than food, and your body more than clothing?... are you not of more value than they?" "But seek first the kingdom of God and his righteousness, and all these things shall be added to you." (Matthew 6:25, 26, 33).

In the greatest of oppositions and danger, Caleb was not concerned about his wellbeing and provision. His greatest concern was obedience to God's command and the honor of His great and glorious Name.

Even when the nation threatened to stone these spiritual leaders to death, they did not apologize about their stand. The heat of the trials did not melt down their faith and confidence in God. They, like the three Hebrew children in the book of Daniel would have gladly died by stoning rather than bow down to the god of comfort and popularity.

There comes a time in a believer's life when you have to make your stand known even in the midst of great opposition, great pain and even at the thread of death. You need not go looking for trouble or opposition, but if trouble or opposition find you in the service of the Savior, then you will need to stand your ground and let the Lord defend you. Our brother Peter tells us that we ought to consider ourselves blessed when we suffer for Christ (1 Peter 3:14).

> Always remember that the most important thing in the Kingdom of God is His glory.

There are times that the Lord will remove the sources of opposition, but at other times He will allow us to go through the trials when He knows that our perseverance will build our character or bring Him greater glory than our safety. Always remember that the most important thing in the Kingdom of God is His glory. So if He sees that your suffering will bring him greater glory than your safety, then he will let you go through the suffering, but He will still bring you out.

The apostle Peter encourages us to stand firm and even rejoice when we suffer for Christ's sake. "Beloved do not think it strange concerning the fiery trials which is to try you as though some strange thing happened to you; but rejoice to the extent that you partake of Christ's suffering, that when His glory is revealed, you may also be glad with exceeding joy" (1 Peter 4:12-13).

Bless those who oppose you

When the opposition arose we see that Caleb and the other spiritual leaders fell on their faces in order to intercede for the nation of Israel. How easy it would have been to curse these people at such a time. Caleb and his friends could not consider cursing the people. Instead they opted to intercede for the very people who wanted to stone them! This should be our attitude towards those who fight and oppose us.

We cannot afford to point an accusing finger to those who have fought and opposed us. Paul reminds us that some of us were exactly as those that we now see as sinners. "And that is what some of you were. But you were washed, you were sanctified, you were justified in the name of the Lord Jesus Christ and by the Spirit of our God (1 Corinthians 6:11). We, too, were sinners and probably acted the same way or even worse. It is by God's marvelous grace that we got saved, and by the very same grace those who oppose us can be saved, especially when we respond to the opposition in a godly manner. Our place should be in the gap. Just like in the days of Ezekiel, God is still looking for someone with a Caleb-like spirit to stand in the gap and intercede for the nations (Ezekiel 22:30).

You need not go looking for trouble or opposition, but if trouble or opposition find you in the service of the Savior, then you will need to stand your ground and let the Lord defend you.

Even of today, God has no pleasure at the death of the wicked. He would rather that they turn from their wicked ways and receive healing, forgiveness, and redemption from his Hand (Ezekiel 33:11). God's desire is for all sinners to come to repentance (2 Peter 3:9).

I love to read stories of great prayer warriors. These are men and women who spend long periods of time interceding for the salvation of a particular group of people or their own communities until they get a breakthrough.

Such a man was John Hyde, also nicknamed "Praying Hyde." This man prayed for the salvation of India and spent many hours, sometimes whole nights or days in prayers. (Carre, *Praying Hyde*, 78) At first he had very little result, but he kept on praying and believing God for souls. If we will experience results in our labors, we will need people with the passion of "Praying Hyde." We need men and women who will not give up until the answer comes.

Consideration for others

Another great characteristic of Caleb was his appreciation and consideration for others in the nation of Israel as well as in his tribe of Judah. First we note that he comes to Joshua requesting that his tribe be remembered in the distribution of land. He comes to Joshua 45 years after they had entered the land of promise, and yet he was among the top names in Israel. How come he waited until almost everybody else had received their inheritance? It seems that Caleb's faith did not waver with the passing of years. He believed that God's promise to him would be realized in God's time. He did not rash things. He had learned to wait upon the Lord. He waited patiently while others were receiving their land and yet unlike everybody else God had personally promised to bless him (Numbers 14:24). Almost everybody else would have argued, "Now that I was among the two faithful spies who actually led you to the land of promise, I deserve to be given the first portion." Caleb waited for forty-five years to receive his inheritance. He considered the joy of others in the God's kingdom as his joy. What attitudes do we have when we observe others in the kingdom of God prospering or doing better than ourselves?

Shared Victory, Shared Joy

When Caleb reappears in the political life of the Israelites, we find him presenting the needs of the tribe of Judah. He did not just ask for his own land. He came representing others. He felt that the victory of the tribe of Judah was his victory too. He did not visit Joshua at night alone and demand his rights. Of course if anybody in Israel qualified to be favored with land, wealth, and power; that person was Caleb. However, he did not push his personal rights. He came bringing his brothers of the tribe of Judah with him.

Caleb's story makes me wonder how the countries of Africa and South America would have developed if the national leaders would have behaved like Caleb. Contrary to Caleb's way of life, we find that most of these leaders quickly amassed lots of wealth for themselves, most times at the expense and destruction of their whole nation. One of the best examples is one of the previous presidents of Congo by the name Mobutu Seseko. He pillaged his nation and became one of the wealthiest men in the world. He had eleven palaces and lots of other properties while the nation continued to get poorer (McCullum, *Africa's Broken*, 9-15). That nation has not recovered to date.

However, there were a few of these African leaders who had the right perspective in leadership. One such leader was Kwame Nkrumah of Ghana. When the nation of Ghana gained its independence from Britain, the Ghanaians were elated and rejoiced at having the colonial rule and chains broken after a very long time of oppression. However, even with this joy, Nkurumah showed his nation that the freedom of one African nation was not sufficient. He would not rest until the rest of Africa was free. To Nkrumah Africa was not free until every inch of Africa was free. He continually campaigned for the unity of the young African nations (*I Speak*, 125-134, 175-177). What a wise visionary leader! Such a spirit of Pan-Africanism was strong among a few of the fathers of the African nations, but unfortunately in most cases that spirit did not match the spirit of greed, power and self-aggrandizement which literally wrecked most of these African nations.

The spirit of caring for one another is the spirit we find in Caleb and is the spirit that the Lord expects each of us to have. We are called to think of the welfare of others, beginning with those within the fellowship of the saints (Galatians 6:10). This is what the scripture means when it says, Bear one another's burdens, and so fulfill the law of Christ (Galatians 6:2) and *"Be* hospitable to one another without grumbling. As each one has received a gift, minister it to one another, as good stewards of the manifold grace of God" (1 Peter 4:9-10).

Each of us Counts

I remember hearing a story, which I later read, regarding one man who held one of the junior positions at NASA. President John F. Kennedy visited this space center at Cape Canaveral in the early 60's. As the president toured the complex, he met a number of people and asked each of them what they did at the space center? Each of them explained their position and job. When he came to this one man who was a sweeper, he asked the same questions, "What do you do here?" This man smiled and replied, "Mr. President, I'm helping to put a man on the moon." (Eric Garner). This man understood team work. He understood that it did not matter how high or low his position was; the important thing was that he was involved in the work that got the whole project complete. He understood that even though he was not a scientist, and all he did was sweep the floors, the whole project would not be complete without sweeping!

This is God's call for each and every one of us. Whatever part you play in the kingdom of God is important, as long as you learn to value and appreciate what others are doing. God calls us to be concerned about the welfare of the others in the body of Christ. Actually the word of God advices us to be careful how we treat even those who are weak in the faith. Paul advised the believers to watch how they treat those who are weak. "Brethren, if a man is overtaken in any trespass, you who are spiritual restore such a one in a spirit of gentleness, considering yourself lest you also be tempted" (Galatians 6:1). He also advised the Corinthians to watch that they did not eat meat sacrificed to idols if it would become a stumbling block to the weaker saints (1 Corinthians 8:1-13).

Settling Gradually

For Caleb, the settling in the land of Canaan was gradual. For some reason the Lord made him wait for forty-five years, before his family would feel settled in the land of promise. I really don't know whether Caleb had other children because we know that his daughter was Achsah who got married to Othniel Caleb's nephew, but I wonder what explanation he gave to his children all these many years. How do you explain God's goodness and faithfulness to your family when it seems that He has not quite fulfilled all the promises He has made to you? Do you get discouraged, frustrated, and then give up? Not so for Caleb. He believed that He who promised was also faithful and would eventually come through for him. He understood that delays are not denials. There are times that God seems to allow these long waiting periods to test our faith and our character.

If you have been waiting anxiously and patiently for a long time, know that our heavenly Father has not forgotten you. Actually, He has purposely made you wait that long because He knows your strength and ability. God knows you well enough that He will trust you to make it even after a long wait. Some people reading this are wondering, "Is the writer talking about me or some other more saintly believers?" Indeed, I am talking about you! You are special and precious to our loving heavenly Father. If God can trust us with the preaching of the gospel, then He can trust us for many other things. The gospel of Christ is the power of God unto salvation (Romans 1:16). God has opted not to use any other method to reach the lost humanity. He has entrusted this great responsibility to us. He actually trusts us to be His vessels to touch the world for Him.

The Fullness of Time

Just like the case with Caleb, God trusts you to stand strong and patiently until, "the fullness of time." Have you noticed how often the scriptures talks of the fullness of time? Indeed, God has a "fullness of time" for each and every one of us. These "fullness of times" are not the same. To some people the "fullness of time" comes faster than for others. Other people wait much longer.

When the fullness of time came Caleb received his inheritance, but not alone. Caleb would not consider enjoying his blessing alone. He came to Joshua with the rest of the tribe of Judah.

A Caleb-like believer or leader is one who does not rejoice that he is the only one living in a certain upscale lifestyle or neighborhood. He does not rejoice in the fact that he drives a better vehicle than all his brothers and sisters or that he has a better job or business than those close to him. Caleb's spirit will desire to see the other brothers and sisters prosper. Such a person will seek the good of the less fortunate in the body of Christ. He or she will sacrifice so that one other person will be lifted to the next level.

Even if you will need to praise the Lord at every step of elevation, don't ever be tempted to think that you got to that place because you are better than others. There are millions of people who spent as much time in school as you did. Others worked even harder than you and got better grades than you in school, and yet they are not doing as good in business or in jobs as you are. God's grace and mercy has brought you to your present position. Only He and He alone should receive the glory for your elevation and success.

I know that there could be someone reading this chapter who is almost giving up. You feel like the Lord has forgotten you. While you are in that mind set, take a moment and think about Caleb. The Lord had called him His servant and declared that Caleb had followed Him whole-heartedly when Caleb was about forty years old (Numbers 14:24). Think about it, if the Lord were to declare that you are special and that you have followed Him whole-heartedly, nobody would question or doubt your holiness or commitment. God sees our hearts and when He declares that someone is faithful, definitely he is faithful. He declared Caleb to be faithful and yet had him wait for forty-five years before releasing his inheritance to him.

I have often gone to the Lord in repentance for being anxious and impatient. I like it when the Lord releases His blessings instantly or in shorter periods of time, but most often He does not. I have learned over the years the need to wait patiently for Him. "I waited patiently for the Lord; and He inclined to me, and heard my cry. He also brought me out of a horrible pit, out of the miry clay, and set my feet upon a rock, and established my steps. He has put a new song in my mouth–Praise to our God; many will see it and fear, and will trust in the Lord (Psalm 40: 1-3).

In Hebrews 6:12, the scriptures admonishes us not to be lazy, but rather to learn from those who through faith and patience inherited the promises (Hebrews 6:12). Even though faith is the key to all doors in the spiritual realm, we need to add patience to our faith. We need to understand that even though God will meet our needs according to His riches in glory by Christ Jesus (Philippians 4:18), He will come at His own time, and He's never late. We need to trust the Lord knows the best for us. He knows the right season for whatever we need.

Armstrong Cheggeh

Lesson from Chapter 4

FROM THE STORY of Joshua and Caleb we are reminded that sometimes the truth is in the hands of the minority.

If you have been opposed and attacked for standing for the truth; please understand that you are not alone and neither are you the first to be opposed and ostracized for the sake of truth. Actually the bible states clearly that is you choose godliness, you shall definitely be opposed.

God has promised to give us the wisdom and even the words to say when we find ourselves in situations of oppositions and persecutions.

"El-Elohe-Israel," the God of Israel has never lost a battle, and is not about to lose any. Hold on to His everlasting arms and you will always have the victory.

There are times that God may ask you to do something that does not seem to make sense at the time. You are left with the choice of either ignoring the command because it does not seem to make sense or just obeying it and leaving the results to the Lord.

It is impossible to experience the abundant life when we allow the spirit of fear, doubts, and unbelief to reign in our spirits.

There are times that the Lord will remove the sources of opposition, but at other times He will allow us to go through the trials when He knows that our perseverance will build our character or bring Him greater glory than our safety.

If you have been waiting anxiously and patiently for a long time, know that our heavenly Father has not forgotten you. Actually, He has purposely made you wait that long because He knows your strength and ability. God knows you well enough that He will trust you to make it even after a long wait.

A Caleb-like believer or leader is one who does not rejoice that he is the only one living in a certain upscale lifestyle or neighborhood. He does rejoice in the fact that he drives a better vehicle than all his brothers and sisters or that he has a better job or business than those close to him. Caleb's spirit will desire to see the other brothers and sisters prosper.

Chapter 5

What Kind of Legacy: A Curse or a Blessing?

AS WE CONTINUE with the subject of leaving behind a righteous legacy, I have chosen to get out our main story in order to share with the readers a few true stories–some from the bible and some from history that will speak to us on the issue of legacy. I will first share stories of three people who left regrettable legacies and then share two stories of people who left legacies that were a blessing to other people. Actually, one of the legacies is blessing people in the Christendom even to this day.

These Three left a Bad Legacy

The Man of God Who Left Debts

In the book 2 Kings 4:1 we find a very interesting story. The bible says, "A certain woman of the wives of the sons of the prophets cried out to Elisha, saying, "Your servant my husband is dead, and you know that your servant feared the Lord. And the creditor is coming to take my two sons to be his slaves."

Here was as servant of God who had died and left a large debt that would have caused his children to become slaves. Can you imagine this happening to a prophet's family? This was not just an ordinary person. Everyone in his village, including Prophet Elisha knew this man. Actually, we know he was a real man of God because even Elisha did not argue with the prophet's wife. He did not answer this woman with words like, "I knew your husband, but he was a good for nothing, and was not committed to the things of God." On the contrary we see this senior prophet going into action immediately. He cared deeply for this widow and her children. The only positive thing about the man of God who had died was that even though he had left debts, and may have not have been a good investor, at least he had a good testimony, in that Elisha did not seem to doubt the fact the man had lived for the Lord during his lifetime.

Elisha performed the miracle that almost every preacher has preached about. By the anointing of this great man of God oil was increased to fill all the jars that this widow and her boys would gather. The miracle happened and the oil was increased. The widow was able to not only sell and pay the debts that had been accumulated by the husband, but also had enough to use in the house and sell for food. The prophet told her, "Go, sell the oil and pray your debt; and you and your sons live on the rest" (2 Kings 4:7).

The reason I am narrating this story here is to remind every believer, and especially the preachers of the gospel of the need to be faithful and invest well in the things that the Lord has entrusted to us. It would be such a shameful thing for a servant of God to die and then have his children sold because of the debts he left while he lived. Of course we will not talk of being sold into open slavery since slavery was abolished years ago. I am referring to it as "open slavery," because it is known that in some of the African and Arabic nations there are still cases of hidden slavery.

My point here is to remind ourselves that even though our children may not be sold to slavery, it is possible to leave them in a situation that would compare closely to slavery. Matthew Henry brings to our attention that this prophet does not seem to have left his debts because of prodigality luxury or riotous living since he is said to have been someone who feared the Lord (Henry, 563). There are some people who may not be living careless lives in as far as loving God and serving Him, but who unfortunately fail to see the need to invest for the future. The idea here is not necessarily to become millionaires, but rather being careful that when we go to be with the Lord we do not leave our families in debts.

In a later chapter I have discussed the need for every fellowship or denomination to come up with projects or programs of honoring those who serve them when they get older. Every church and ministry in the free world ought to have a solid retirement program for their ministers. What I mean by saying "in the free world," is because some countries don't have the freedom of worship, and so some of the churches in those countries are house churches that are concerned about survival than retirement benefits.

> *There are some people who may not be living careless lives in as far as loving God and serving Him, but who unfortunately fail to see the need to invest for the future.*

However, in the free world, we need to always know that we will not always be young and strong. As we age we may not always be able to do what we did while we were younger. We should therefore, seek for ways and means to invest for the future. Of course one of the ways to make this investment is to educate your children. Educating your children is one way to make sure that after you've gone to heaven, your sons and daughters will not suffer.

I still remember a preacher who died in my country that was living in a very prestigious neighborhood. The only problem was that the large house he and his family occupied, while he lived was not his, but rented. When he died his family had to leave that large house, and could not afford living anywhere close to that neighborhood.

This particular preacher and many others that I've observed would rather pay hefty rental fees than purchase a smaller house in a lower middle class neighborhood. They are overly concerned about the praise of men. They would rather live in large homes that are not theirs for many years because they have to appear rich! Actually, I thought this was only in Africa but I've seen this same spirit in America. Such families get into all kinds of problems if the money-maker dies.

In this book I will not discuss much about making money or investments because there are so many books on the same. Mine is only to remind the believers not to be like the man of God, who left his children in the hands of the creditors. Please be very careful not to leave your family in the hands of the creditors.

A Man that was cursed by a Whole Village

I want to share another story that took place in my own country. In a place called Murang'a in Kenya a certain man died. When the day of the funeral came something very strange happened.

The Kikuyu people normally have very long funeral services. Normally funeral services are what the Western world calls "Grave-side" services. In the Western world those services don't take even half an hour. I have presided over funerals in America especially when I was a Chaplain with the Hospice of the Bluegrass. I couldn't believe how short American funeral services were. I had to learn quickly to make them real short because I knew that if I conducted the funeral service as I would in Africa, these Americans might as well leave me to bury the dead by myself!

The point I'm making is that Africans love their funeral services. Sometimes they take four to five hours just in the funeral service! Recently I attended the funeral of one of our family friend's mother. The local Catholic priest preached for an hour and a half, and this was after about ten people had eulogized the lady who had died. The funeral began around noon and ended around five in the evening and nobody left. That's the way we conduct our funeral in most places in Africa. We just love our funeral services!

In this kind of background you would expect every time you

Leaving Behind a Righteous Legacy

go to a funeral, to spend at least three or more hours. However, when the man I mentioned above died in the area of Murang'a, the funeral service broke the record in being one of the shortest funeral services in the whole region.

When the Master of Ceremonies stood up he noticed nobody was listed to eulogize the man. In many African funerals we usually have to limit how many people can talk because everybody wants to say somethings. In this particular funeral nobody wanted to say anything. The relatives and family friends just kept quite even when the invitation was given to say something about the deceased.

Finally, one of the brave souls in the family who had known the man who had died for many years and was a close relative stood up. He walked to the casket and pointed at it. He said, "All of you know that we of the Kikuyu tribe love farming. When we find a piece of land that has Kikuyu grass called "Kigombe, we feel much better because this kind is easier to deal with. When you dig the Kigombe grass for the first time, it is gone for good!

The man continued with his story: "However, we do have the other kind of grass... He stopped for a moment for effect, and asked do you know that other grass that is stubborn? The whole congregation answered, "Yes, it is called Thangari!" He then asked them, "When you have Thangari in your farm what do you do?" They responded that the farmer had to do a harder job and dig much deeper to the roots of the Thangari. When someone got to the roots he got it all and also shook the soil from this grass and sometimes they even moved it away and burned it.

Then he added, "When we have Thangari in any farm, we seek to destroy it and wish that it will be gone completely, and never to return." He used a Kikuyu word which mean, "May it be eradicated forever." That word is, "*Irohuka.*" He then pointed to the casket and said, "the man in this casket is Thangari! I want you to help me say "*Irohuka!*" (May it be destroyed forever!) The whole village, including the family of this man joined-in to curse the very memory of this man who had been a terror to his family and many others. His family was very glad that he was gone!

Again, the question I have for each of the readers is, "What kind of memory will your family and friends have of you? What kind of legacy will you leave behind?

Died to no one's Sorrow

My final story of the people who left bad legacies is to be found in the book of 2 Chronicles chapter twenty-one. This story interestingly is about one of the sons of a very godly King. He was the sons of Jehoshaphat. I do not know of any preacher of the gospel who has not preached about the greatness of Jehoshaphat. Personally, I have preached many times from 2 Chronicles chapter twenty. I love the story of Jehoshaphat's faith and his prayer when he realized that his enemies were much stronger and numerous than his feeble army. I love especially verse twelve, "O our God, will you not judge them? For we have no power against this great multitude that is coming against us; nor do we know what to do, but our eyes are upon you." God responded to Jehoshaphat's faith marvelously and gave Israel a great victory.

Even with such a great story, Jehoram, one of his sons made a grave mistake. He married the daughter of King Ahab. Can you imagine Jezebel being your mother-in-law!

It's still possible to have godly parents and still make mistakes. God holds us responsible as we raise our sons and daughters, but when they are grown, it is upon them to make choices on what they want to become. The parents cannot continue making choices for the children after they have become adults. In this case, Johoram made wrong choices even though he was raised in a godly family.

Jehoram became king after the death of his father Jehoshaphat. This young man did not follow his father's example. First he married from the wrong family. His wife was the daughter of Ahab, one of the most ungodly kings in Israel. His wife's name "Jezebel" was almost synonymous with "control spirit" or just a cunning, conniving or manipulative spirit.

We do not know exactly the influence of Jehoram's wife or in-laws, but the Bible makes it clear that his evil ways came about because of his relationship with the family he married into. "And he walked in the way of the kings of Israel, just as the house of Ahab had done, for he had the daughter of Ahab as a wife; and he did evil in the sight of the Lord" (2 Chronicles 21:6).

As soon as he got well established in the kingdom, he killed all his brothers and all the influential leaders in Israel (2 Chronicles 21:4). He seemed to have been a very insecure leader. He also strengthened idolatry in Israel and also caused the defeat of the armies of Israel because of his sins (2 Chronicles 21:8-11, 14-15).

Jehoram misbehaved to the extent that when he finally died, the nation refused to bury him in the tombs of the Kings. The Bible says that he died, "to no one's sorrow." (2 Chronicles 21:20). This is a terrible ending. When he died nobody wept for him. Nobody cared that he had died. What a legacy of shame!

All these three people left legacies of shame, pain, and defeat. Their stories are the kind you don't want to identify with. You don't want to leave a legacy of debt like the man of God in 2 Kings 4:1 or even be cursed by a whole village for having lived a reckless, irresponsible life. I pray that none of the readers of this book will die, "to no one's sorrow."

Two People with Outstanding Luminous Legacies

First, I want to share a short story in the book of Acts of the Apostles. There was a godly woman by the name Dorcas or Tabitha who lived in the seaport town of Joppa (Acts **9:36-39**). She loved the Lord with all her heart. Actually, the first things we are told about this precious saint was that she was a disciple. This is important because before we can be involved in acts of charity and benevolence, we need to become disciples of our Lord Jesus Christ. Dorcas was a disciple. Our faith in God should be the foundation upon which all our works are established.

Dorcas was greatly involved in the lives of the other saints, especially the widows in the community. In a day and time when the emphasis of many preachers is on how to amass a lot of wealth and build the greatest of mansions on earth and if possible own personal jets, here is a story of a woman who used her wealth to touch others with the love of Jesus. May God give the church many Dorcases.

However, I want to clarify something here in case someone categorizes me with those who have a poverty mentality or those who glorify poverty. Personally I do not see anything wrong with a believer living in a beautiful large house and driving a nice car. The point here is that we should not only be concerned about our personal or family comfort, but should constantly be involved in the lives of the needy people in our communities. None can solve all the problems in our communities, but we should be found doing whatever we can to alleviate poverty among those that are close to us, especially in the household of faith (Galatians 6:10).

We do not know many things about Dorcas, but all we know is that when she died, her village and all who knew her grieved for her. She left such a vacuum in the community because of her involvement in the lives of the widows in her village. Like Caleb, this woman did not live for herself. She had a living testimony and served the Lord whole-heartedly and also touched many lives in her village.

From all accounts she was not a preacher. She was, as it were, just an ordinary Christian, but who did extra-ordinary ministry among the needy in her community. The life of Dorcas shows us that we do not have to be preachers to touch people's lives. In my first book, I said, "There is nothing secular in God's kingdom. As long as you honor the Lord in that which you do, then your job or profession becomes sacred as the pastoral work or the bishopric! (*Developing*, 7). In Colossians 3:23-24, Paul tells us, "And whatever you do, do it heartily, as to the Lord and not to men, knowing that from the Lord you will receive the reward of the inheritance; for you serve the Lord Christ.

When Dorcas died the whole village mourned for this dear saint. The believers knew that Peter was in Lydda, a nearby village and sent for him. When Peter arrived, he made the people get out of the house and knelt and prayed that God would raise Dorcas from the dead. The Lord honored the prayers of Peter. However, I don't think the Dorcas was raised from the dead just because of Peter's faith. It was more because of the life, testimony and the impact that Dorcas had left in her village. The Bible says, "… And all the widows stood by him weeping, showing the tunics and garments which Dorcas had made while she was with them (Acts 9:39b).

When Peter raised Dorcas from the dead, the miracle not only pleased the widows in that they now would continue to have their friend Dorcas with them, and also benefit from her ministry, but this miracle also caused many to come to faith in Christ (Acts 9:42). Thus the congregation at Joppa grew both in numbers and also in faith because of the faith and work of Dorcas. Actually, the Bible says that the Apostle remained in Joppa for a long time because of the impact of this miracle.

Think about it. How many people had died in Joppa before Dorcas' death? How many had caused such grieve and outcry from the widows? Probably none. The life of Dorcas was lived in such a way that her passing meant a lot to the whole village. She knew her calling and purpose and pursued it to the best of her ability.

Her life should speak to each of us; first to seek the Lord to know exactly what our calling and purpose is. After we have found out what our calling and purpose is, the next step is to pursue it to the best of our ability and to the glory of God. The scriptures tells us, "Whatever your hand finds to do, do *it* with your might" (Ecclesiastes 9:10).

If Dorcas had only been involved in the affairs of her own household, we most likely would never have heard of her. We know of her because she not only loved the Lord, but also lived for the other saints. How about you and I? What impact will we leave in the churches, villages, or towns where we live? If the Lord called you home today, who would miss you and what impact would you live behind?

Armstrong Cheggeh

A Life that impacted Many Generations

Our final story in this section is of Jonathan Edwards who is believed to be one of the greatest and most profound American Theologians and philosophers of all time. His name and theological stand has become such a force that scores of great scholars have sought to know the mind of this great genius. Crisp and Sweeny observe, "Today, there is an intellectual industry devote to furtherance of Edwardsian scholarship, aided by completion of the Yale letterpress edition of Edward's works, and its online, open-access counterpart" (After, 6).

Jonathan lived in a time when every settlement in American was required to have at least one learned, orthodox minister of the gospel in order to qualify for charter (Dodds, *Marriage*, 27). So, the position of a town minister was such a lofty position. Jonathan was not only a city preacher in Northampton, Massachusetts, but more a nation-wide minister in that his preaching and teaching influenced most of the preachers of his day. Of course his message entitled, "Sinners in the hand of an angry God," is one of the best known sermons in Christendom.

Jonathan is also known as one of the greatest fathers of the Great awakening that took place in America beginning in the early part of the seventeen hundreds. Winslow describes the impact of the revival, "This Revival, or rather series of revivals, vitalized afresh the religious experiences of the average man, and gave to the doctrines and forms of the church an intensely new personal meaning" (*Jonathan Edwards*, 165).

Jonathan was raised in a godly home. His father, the Rev. Timothy Edwards, was the pastor of the Congregational Church in Windsor Farms, Connecticut, where he pastored for sixty years. His mother was Esther Stoddard who also was raised in a very godly minister's home. Her father, Solomon Stoddard was the pastor at the Congregational Church in Northampton, Massachusetts from 1672 to 1729. Jonathan Edwards took over as senior pastor after his grandfather death.

Jonathan became a minister in his early twenties, and married a Sarah Pierrepont of New Haven whose father was the first minister in this town. She too, was a very godly woman who was deeply committed to spiritual things. Winslow describes her as, having a "single-mindedness of endeavor which set her apart even from those of her own age" (*Jonathan Edwards*, 111).

I bring the story of Jonathan Edwards here not only because he was a great preacher who left a great ministerial legacy that most of the future generations of preachers have benefited from, but more because of the family he and his wife Sarah raised, and the kind of impact his family has had on many generations. First, I want to share a little bit about his family life and then present to the readers the luminous lineage of this great couple. I want to share a little bit of their devotional life, as well as their involvement with their children, to show that a great legacy does not just happen. A powerful legacy that, impacts future generations calls for very real godly decisions and real choices as to how we need to live and how we need to raise our families.

Family altar was such a valuable time in the home of the Edwards. Not only did Edward himself wake up early for personal devotion, but he also involved the whole family and everyone who might be staying or visiting with them. "So everyone in the house was routed out, even in the dark winter dawns, for prayers by candlelight. With the servants joining in, they all heard a chapter from the Bible and asked God's blessing on the day ahead" (Dodds, *Marriage*, 33).

He emphasized that our family altar should come first and foremost, more as a foundation to our Christian and church lives. "Every Christian family ought to be as it were a little church, consecrated to Christ, and wholly influenced and governed by his rules. And family education and order are some of the chief of the means of grace. If these fail, all other means are likely to prove ineffectual. If these are duly maintained, all the means of grace will be like to prosper and be successful" (Kimnach, *The Sermons*, 236) (Faust and Johnson, *Jonathan*, 197).

According to Jonathan Edwards, church life makes no sense if it does not begin at home. If all believers would emphasize this aspect of their lives, then our Christian lives would become much more vibrant and most likely many children impacted for eternity.

Jonathan seems to have been very aware of God's holiness and also his own spiritual frailties and sin and thus sought the Lord regularly (Dodds, *Marriage*, 34). He also gave himself to much study both for his own spiritual growth and for the purpose preaching effectively. "Because he held a high view of the pulpit, he believed it was his duty to thoroughly study the scriptures and deliver to his congregation the mind of Christ (Vaughan, *A Divine*, 2007).

> A powerful legacy that, impacts future generations calls for very real godly decisions and real choices as to how we need to live and how we need to raise our families.

Jonathan Edwards loved his wife dearly. "Edwards, though an absent-minded father, gave his children another important thing: complete confidence that their parents loved each other. Sarah sat next to her husband at the table, and he treated her with great courtesy. She, in turn leaned on him" (Dodds, *Marriage*, 48). Piper observe, "Jonathan and Sarah's affection for each other and the regular family devotional routine were strong blocks in the children's foundation" (*A God*, 64).

Not only did Jonathan and Sarah love and treat their children in honor, but also "approached the discipline of their children as a united pair, and this may be one reason why the children, in turn, married happily" (Dodds, *Marriage*, 48). Edwards also made sure that he gave one hour every day to the children and also would often have one of the children accompany him during his travels (Piper, *A God*, 64).

Sarah herself was such a godly woman that all who knew her talked of her good graces and her commitment to the things of God. Someone described her as "the supporter and protector and home-builder for Jonathan Edwards, whose philosophy and passion for God is still vital 300 years after his birth" (Piper, 76).

She also cared greatly for her children, and was also a great disciplinarian. "She had an excellent way of governing her children; she knew how to make them regard and obey her cheerfully, without loud angry words, much less heavy blows. She seldom punished them; and in speaking to them, used gentle and pleasant words. If any correction was necessary, she did not administer it in a passion; and when she had occasion to reprove and rebuke she would do it in a few words, without warmth (that is vehemence) and noise..." (Dodds, 42-43).

It was noted by all who visited the Edward's home that their children were well disciplined. "All visitors seem to have been impressed that eleven children managed to be lively and individual as personalities, yet could act courteously with one another and function as a coordinated unit" (Dodds, 39).

Due to the godly lives that both Jonathan and Sarah Edwards lived, and the fact that they cared deeply on how they raised their large family, the future of their children and their descendant was determined as we shall see.

Thousands of Jonathan and Sarah Edwards's descendants became prominent citizens in the United States. Both Jonathan and Sarah did not live long lives. Jonathan died at 55 and Sarah died at 49 and yet their impact in both their family and Christendom is phenomenal. This shows us that sometimes it is not how long we live, but rather what kind of lives we live. Some people may live very short lives and leave such a great impact in their communities, while others live for a century and yet not leave a notable impact.

In 1900 an American educator and pastor A.E. Winship studied the lives of 1400 of the Sarah and Jonathan Edwards descendants and compared their lives with the lives of the descendants of another man by the name Max Jukes who had lived in the same time period as Jonathan Edwards, and did not care about godliness and serving the Lord. Max Jukes was not his real name; the writers changed his name to protect his descendants since these were real people living in the USA.

The question here is what kind of impact does an individual leave behind if he or she lives a godly life and is committed to serving the Lord faithfully and being an example to his community in family matters? Will godly decisions today determine what the future will be like for someone's descendants? Could it be that like the promise to Caleb, God does indeed bless the lives of the future descendants of those who love the Him and serve Him whole-heartedly?

First, I want to begin with Max Juke's family. Pastor Winship studied 1,200 of the descendants of this New York Dutchman. Almost all Juke's descendants were in a pitiable state many years after this ungodly man had died. Actually only twenty of them out of the 1,200 descendants had any gainful employment (Dodds, 37). The following was the state of all the other descendant of Max Jukes:

> 310 of them died as paupers.
>
> 150 were criminals.
>
> 7 were murderers.
>
> 100 were drunkards.
>
> More than half of the women were prostitutes.
>
> His Descendants cost the state one and a quarter million dollars (This was a lot of money at that time).

As for the descendants of Sarah and Jonathan Edwards, their story was completely different. God's blessing and presence seemed to have accompanied all his descendants. His descendants included the following:

> 13 college presidents
>
> 65 professors, including three college presidents (Timothy Dwight, Jonathan Edwards, Jr, and Merrill Edwards Gates).
>
> 100 lawyers and a dean of a law school
>
> 30 judges
>
> 66 physicians and a dean of a medical school
>
> 80 holders of public office, including three US Senators,

mayors of three large cities, governors of three states, a Vice-President of the United States (Aaron Burr), and a controller of the United States Treasury.

Jonathan and Sarah Edwards were also ancestors of, First Edith.

They had written over 135 books and edited eighteen journals and periodicals. One of these publishers was Frank Doubleday.

Many had entered the ministry.

Over 100 were missionaries and others were on mission boards. (Dodds, 38-39) (Vaughan, 212-213).

While the family of the man who did not honor the Lord cost the government lots of money, the descendants of Sarah and Edward Jonathan, "cost the country nothing in pauperism, in crime, in hospital or asylum service; on the contrary, it represents the highest usefulness" (Dodds, 38-39).

Who can argues with the fact that, "the memory of the just is blessed" (Proverbs 10:7). Did this just happen? Was this just a coincidence that a particular Christian couple had such a legacy? I don't think so! The spiritual choices we make in our lives make a difference not only in our own lives, but also in the lives of all the people in our families and in the people that we encounter every day.

These true stories should challenge each of us to be extremely careful how we live. Our decisions today will definitely affect our children and other people around us. What kind of influence do you want to have on your future generations? Like Caleb, may our decisions be that we will serve the Lord whole-heartedly so much so that our future generation will inherit the "land" of blessings and stability.

Armstrong Cheggeh

Lessons from Chapter 5

AS WE AGE we may not always be able to do what we did while we were younger. We should therefore, seek for ways and means to invest for the future, so that we don't struggle as much.

God holds us responsible as we raise our sons and daughters, but when they are grown, it is upon them to make choices on what they want to become.

Before we can be involved in acts of charity and benevolence, we need to become disciples of our Lord Jesus Christ. Dorcas was a disciple. Our faith in God should be the foundation upon which all our works are established.

The life of Dorcas shows us that we do not have to be preachers to touch people's lives.

Dorcas was raised from the dead not only because of Peter's faith, but more because of the life, testimony and the impact that she had left in her village.

After we have found out what our calling and purpose is, the next step is to pursue it to the best of our ability and to the glory of God.

A powerful legacy that, impacts future generations calls for very real godly decisions and real choices as to how we need to live and how we need to raise our families.

According to Jonathan Edwards, church life makes no sense if it does not begin at home.

Sometimes it is not how long we live, but rather what kind of lives we live. Some people may live very short lives and leave such a great impact while others live for a century and yet not leave a notable impact.

The spiritual choices we make in our lives make a difference not only in our own lives, but also in the lives of all the people in our families and in the people that we encounter every day.

Like Caleb, may our decisions be that we will serve the Lord whole-heartedly so much so that our future generation will inherit the "land" of blessings and stability.

Chapter 6

In Search of True Friends

WHENEVER WE HAVE had friends in our home, I find myself thanking the Lord for, "the gift of friendship." Good friends are a great asset. You cannot exchange them with anything. I have come across people who have no friends, or who are very poor in establishing friendships, and indeed they end up living comparatively unhappy lives. Life without friends is dull. Friends and friendship are a great spice to life. Our brother John Townsend writes of how valuable these relationships are. "Life is essentially about relationships, and it is empty without relationships. This is especially trues with the leader" (*Leadership*, 113).

True friendship is one of the characteristics we want to glean from Caleb's life. We find in the story of Joshua and Caleb a friendship that lasted a lifetime. At the edge of the land of Canaan, Joshua and Caleb joined hands as they stood against the unbelief of the other ten spies and indeed the whole nation of Israel. This opposition and suffering may have cemented their relationship. We find them forty-five years later relating on the things of God. What a friendship!

The life of Caleb impressed not only the religious leaders of Israel or the tribe of Judah which he led for over forty-five years, but also impressed the Lord Himself. It is good to honor and please the people around you, but it is far better to please our heavenly Father. Caleb, through his life, sought to please the Lord before pleasing men. However, even with pleasing the Lord, he also established strong relationships with other leaders in Israel.

One of the most important lessons learned from the life of Caleb is that of true friendships. First we encounter these two friends as they leave the Israelite camp to go and spy the land of the Canaanites. These two faithful men stood together for truth, when their report differed from the other ten spies. Their stand almost cost them their lives.

We do not know much about Caleb in the next forty-five years, but the next time we see him he is a polished leader of the tribe of Judah (Joshua 14:6).

The way Caleb addressed Joshua shows that his life and testimony had been consistent. He says, "And now, behold, the Lord has kept me alive, as He said, these forty-five years, even since the Lord spoke this word to Moses while Israel wandered in the wilderness; and now, here I am this day, eighty-five years old. As yet I am as strong this day as on the day that Moses sent me; just as my strength was then, so now is my strength for war, both for going out and for coming in" (Joshua 14:10-11).

Jesus the Faithful Friend

As I was reading the story of these two great men of God, I wondered what characteristics in their lives brought such stability in their long relationship. First, I thought of the greatest friend there is. The bible says, "A man *who has* friends must himself be friendly, But there is a friend *who* sticks closer than a brother" (Proverbs 18:24). God is the greatest friend we have. God's friendship to us is unique in that He knows us in the best and deepest way there is to know anybody, and yet he loves us just as we are. Just think about it, the Lord knows your weaknesses. He knows exactly how you are and where you've been; where you are right now, and where you shall be, and yet He still loves you. That is why the scriptures say He sticks closer than a brother.

The Lord Jesus Christ told the disciples, "You are my friends if you do what I command. I no longer call you servants, because a servant does not know his master's business. Instead, I have called you friends, for everything that I learned from my Father I have made known to you" (John 15:13-15). Jesus is the purest example of a true friend; for He laid down His life for His friends. What is more, anyone, the whole world over, may become His friend by trusting in Him as his personal savior, being born again and receiving new life in Him (See John 1:12).

That's why it so good to have Jesus as your friend, because when all other friends fail and forsake you, He will always be the one true friend you can count on. He indeed sticks closer than a brother (Proverbs 18:24).

Personally, I have known the truth of these words on several occasions. There are times in leadership when I have had to literally run to this everlasting and faithful friend. Actually, there is no way I would have survived in the ministry for as many years as I have, were it not for this friendship with my Lord.

My sister Mary Nyakiago, who has since gone to be with the Lord, taught me a song that became one of my favorites. This song explains the love of God best:

> *The love of God is greater far*
> *Than tongue or pen can ever tell.*
> *It goes beyond the highest star*
> *And reaches to the lowest hell.*
> *The guilty pair, bowed down with care,*
> *God gave His Son to win;*
> *His erring child He reconciled*
> *And pardoned from his sin.*
>
> *(Frederick M. Lehman, 1917 – Public domain).*

I began the discussion about friendship with our relationship with the Lord because all other friends and friendships can and do fail. So, as we look at what a godly friendship should look like, I wanted us to begin on a solid footing. At least we will always find a place of repose; a place where we can always retreat when other ground becomes sinking sand.

The friendship of Joshua and Caleb was especially established by their common faith. Their friendship and loyalty to the Lord, cemented their friendship. They did not meet in a pub when having a drink and developed their long-lasting friendship. Their friendship began at the altar. Their friendship was based on their greater friendship with the Shepherd of Israel (See Psalm 80:1). Their intimacy with the Father influenced their intimacy with each other. What a blessing it would be if every friendship or relationship began at the altar.

What kinds of friends do you have? What is the foundation upon which your friendship is built? If the answer to these questions is negative, then I would urge you to evaluate your priorities. Jesus taught that knowing Him and having a relationship with Him was much more valuable than the riches of this whole world. "For what will it profit a man if he gains the whole world, and loses his own soul? (Mark 8:36). John advised the early church to be careful how they related to the world. "Do not love the world or the things in the world. If anyone loves the world, the love of the Father is not in him. For all that is in the world—the lust of the flesh, the lust of the eyes, and the pride of life—is not of the Father but is of the world. And the world is passing away, and the lust of it; but he who does the will of God abides forever" (1 John 2:15-17).

> Real love and real friendship calls for some investments. I don't know of any long-lasting relationship that does not call for some giving and sacrifice.

Giving and Sacrifice

Jesus describes his friendship to us this way: "Greater love has no one than this, than to lay down one's life for his friends" (John 15:13). Jesus shows us what real love and real friendship means. The one who really loves can lay his life for his friends. That's real sacrifice. Real love and real friendship calls for some investments.

I don't know of any long-lasting relationship that does not call for some giving and sacrifice.

Let me address especially those of you planning to get married. If you cannot give up something for your beloved, then you need to think twice about your relationship. If your way has to be right and your fiancé's wrong, then probably you don't love deeply enough to get into a life-long relationship. If you have to have your way in the relationship, then probably you really don't care for that particular person.

True relationships call for compromises. Here I do not mean compromising the truth of the gospel, but rather agreeing or coming to a middle ground on different issue of life. Friendships and lasting relationships call for sacrifice. You have to lose some things in order to gain the benefits of a good friendship. For your friendship to gain solidity, you will have to work towards unity and common values. Prophet Amos asked, "Can two walk together, unless they are agreed? (Amos 3:3).

Once in a while young people will reason within themselves that the person they plan to marry will eventually change. They reason that since they believe in God, all it will take is constant prayers and the power of persuasion to change their partner after they get married. This often happens with young people who are in love with someone who is not committed to the way of the cross. If that person has not changed by the time you meet them, and they have not yielded to the Holy Spirit before you begin your life together, then be warned; they may never change. That is why the Scripture admonishes every believer not to be joined with the unbeliever (See 2 Corinthians 6:14). Entry into the marriage covenant is probably where we need to watch and be careful of the kind of decisions we make, then any other institution.

One young lady we knew well married a young man who was not quite committed in things of God. To this day, that man is not living for Christ. He got worse after they got married.

Faithful Friends

Many people take off when you are not exactly what they expected. These are the fair weather friends. They only stick with you when the relationship or circumstances favor them. As soon as they do not receive the benefits they expected from the friendship they take off. Sometimes these are described as the dry leaves of the Fall season. They do not stick around when the weather changes.

True friendship is a relationship entered into by individuals, and is only as good or as close as those individuals choose to make it. Friendship is a choice. A friend is one whom you can completely be yourself with and never fear that he or she will judge you. A friend is someone that you can be open with and confide in. True friendship calls for mutual trust. There has to be reciprocity of trust. Such a relationship then should not be based upon worthiness but upon shared likes, values and full acceptance. Such friends are the kind who will know the person you are and yet love and appreciate you as you are, not the way you should be.

The Absalom's Syndrome: The Sin of Betrayal

The betrayal of a friend or a close relative is probably one of the most painful experiences that someone can go through. However, the betrayal of parents, sons or daughters usually causes greater pain and grief than any other experience in life.

In the Bible such a betrayal took place in the house of King David, who was one of the most beloved leaders in the Bible. David was so great and beloved of God, that the Lord promised him an everlasting throne, which continues in the reign of Christ, who also is referred to as, "The Son of David (Matthew 1:1, Luke 18:38).

Absalom, the son of David, killed his half-brother Amnon for having defiled his sister Tamar. After committing the murder, the young man fled to Geshur and remained there in exile for three years (2 Samuel 13:37-38). He found it easy to flee for safety in Geshur since his mother was raised a princess in the kingdom of Geshur. Eventually, his father allowed him to return home, and kissed him as a sign of welcoming him back home. However, the young man was not satisfied to remain a prince. He wanted the throne!

The seeds of desiring the kingship may have been sown into his mind by his own mother. Most likely she may have told him of how important he was in that he was not only a child of a King, but also a grandson to a King. He was royalty every way you looked at it! How could he not be the most qualified as the next king? He decided he would be king whether his father wanted it or not. He set out to betray his father, and was even willing to have him killed (2 Samuel 17:1-3).

Absalom began enticing the people by speaking in a derogatory manner about his father. He said, "Oh that I were made judge in the land, and everyone who has any suit or cases would come to me; then I would give him justice" (2 Samuel 15:4). Eventually he was able to convince the people that he was better than his father, and literally stole the people's hearts, and threw his father out of his capital city for a while, but God was not with him.

This young man eventually died a miserable death. His long, and beautiful hair was caught in the boughs of a terebinth tree, and he was suspended in midair! When Joab, the commander of David's army found out, he went and immediately killed him, while still hanging in midair (2 Samuel 18:14). Absalom most likely had more soldiers, who were younger and stronger than those of Joab, the Lord still allowed a swift defeat and a painful death for him, because of his disloyalty.

The "Absalom's syndrome," as this betrayal has been referred to, by Bible scholars, is too common in Christian circles. Most betrayals, whether in the church or not, are not from total strangers. It takes some form of knowledge, and intimacy for someone to have the ability to betray another person effectively. The people who betray you are those who have known you for some time.

It is often the people who have studied your personality well, or even known your life well enough to describe your experiences with some intimate details, who can also betray you. Anybody who has known your weaknesses and is familiar with all your "scars," is the one who can turn around and betray you. Judas walked and talked with Christ often. He knew his likes and dislikes. He knew when and where He preferred to go for moments of prayers, and therefore, it was so easy for him to bring the Jewish leaders to Him in the night.

"Judases" are usually people who are very familiar with the ways of the person they betray. David seems to have known such a person when he wrote, "Even my own familiar friend in whom I trusted, who ate my bread, has lifted up his heel against me (Psalm 41:9). In Psalm 55:12-14, he says, "For it is not an enemy who reproaches me; Then I could bear it. Nor is it one who hates me who has exalted himself against me; Then I could hide from him. But it was you, a man my equal, My companion and my acquaintance. We took sweet counsel together, And walked to the house of God in the throng." From these words we note that this friend who betrayed David had been his brother in the Lord. They took sweet counsel together and fellowship with one another. That is a painful betrayal!

Forgiveness and Betrayal

Forgiving someone who has betrayed you is probably the hardest thing in life, and yet the Lord admonishes us to forgive even our enemies (Matthew 5:44). In Ephesians 4:32, Paul tells us, "And be kind to one another, tenderhearted, forgiving one another, even as God in Christ forgave you." I would be wrong to say that such a forgiveness would be easy. Forgiving someone that has betrayed you, especially a close friend or family members is quite an uphill task. Charles R. Gerber reminds us that, "the closer the relationship to the person who hurt you, the more difficult it is to forgive" (Healing, 162). Yet we still have to forgive if we can expect to enjoy the abundant life.

One thing I am certain of is that God will never give us a command that cannot be fulfilled, or one that we are completely unable to obey. The scriptures teach us that his laws are not burdensome (1 John 5:3-4). In other words, whatever God has commanded us to do, He also gives us the grace and ability to fulfill His will in our lives. God also promises that for every temptation that comes our way, He always makes a way of escape (1 Corinthians 10:13). Whatever our loving heavenly Father tells us to do is because His grace will always enable and empower us to obey.

Betrayed by a Close Friend

There are times that we have been hurt by the betrayal of our best friend, or a close family member. Such betrayal surprises or shock us because it is usually unexpected. At those times the greatest temptation is vindictiveness. You feel that since this particular person has hurt you exceedingly, then you want to revenge. However, the Lord tells us in His word that when we suffer, especially for being right, we should rejoice and be exceedingly glad (Matthew 5:10-12). Peter reminds the believers that when we suffer we are following the example of Christ who suffered for the church, and that we should have patience as we serve the Lord (See 1 Peter 2:19-23). When any of us shows perseverance in situations of trials and suffering, it becomes a great testimony to those around us. Many people have been won to Christ by just observing the response of Christians during seasons of great trials or afflictions.

We should be reminded that there are no trials that are a surprise to our loving heavenly Father. He only allows trials that will be a blessing to his children. Our brother Smith Wigglesworth reminds us of the value of trials in our lives. "If you knew the value of them, you would praise God for trials than for anything. It is the trial that is used to purify you; it is the fiery furnace of affliction that God uses to get you in the place where He can use you (*Smith*, 90).

Friendship Spoilers Bad Counsel

King David was one of the greatest, most loving and compassionate leaders in Israel. One of his best friends was Nahash, the king of the Ammonites. When King David learned that his friend Nahash had died he sent a delegation of chosen men with a message of condolence to King Nahash's son, Hanun.

Hanun, on the other hand was ill advised by his counselors, and instead of appreciating David's kindness and neighborliness, he treated David's messengers shamefully. They returned home embarrassed and frustrated because their mission had turned out to be such a negative experience for them and their king.

When I read this story, I decided to include it in this section of "Friendship spoilers." Just think about it, if only King Hanun had good counselors who would have taken the time to study the relationship between their previous leader and David. If only they had taken the time to study David's character. His character would not have allowed him to deal deceitfully with his neighbor. All they needed to study was David's response and treatment to his worst enemy, King Saul. King Saul had on several occasions attempted to destroy him and yet, David had been careful to do that which was right because of his love and honor for the Lord. Even when opportunity availed itself, he would not think of killing Saul.

The wrong advice to King Hanun by his counselors cost many lives of his own soldiers; thousands of lives of the Assyrian soldiers who came out to assist him, and finally it cost him the most helpful, and supportive friendship, which would have been a great asset not only for himself as a person but also for his kingdom. He lost it all because of wrong counsel.

This story teaches us to be very careful of the kinds of friends and counselors we allow into our lives. The friends you allow into your life are of great importance. Just like in this story of King David and King Hanun, there are scores of lives that get destroyed every single day because of the wrong advice given by a friend that is not spiritual or deep in the things of God.

Above Petty Arguments

Any good friendship has to be ready for challenges, fights, and even disagreements. Being friends does not mean that you completely agree on everything. No one in the whole world would think or act exactly like the other. Everybody has their own value systems and none is completely identical to the other. Even brothers and sisters, who have lived together all their lives do not necessarily see eye to eye in everything. We all live by compromise. We love and support each other in spite of our differences. True friendships are rare and need to be taken care of and protected. Nick Cuthbert reaffirms the same idea. "We all need two or three people that we can be real with, without fear of judgment, criticism or breaking confidence" (How to survive, 69). We should see true friendship as a gift from the Father. Stephanie Ford says this of such friendships, "Whatever the case a soul friendship is not only a gift from God but also a vocation of love to be tended with loyalty and care" (Ford, 17).

Even marriage, which is a life-long relationship, is based on lots of compromises. In marriage you choose to love your spouse including the issues or aspects that you do not quite see eye to eye. Life can be extremely difficult if any of us expected our spouses to act exactly as we desired. It would call for one of the spouses to be a robot! We come into a marriage with issues that are embedded into our beings. We call these, "the way someone is wired." For example, if you married someone that is an introvert and you are an extrovert, you may just have to learn to live with each other instead of trying to change one another.

Viral Friends

I found myself smiling as I read Tom E. Eisenman's book, *The Accountable Man*. He describes a group of people who seem to be bent on negativity, and who also desire to spread it around. He says, "In every fellowship it seems, there are men and women who are like viruses looking for host cells. He warns the believers. "If we are not wise, we can open our lives to the people who do not have a godly agenda" (43).

The older I get the more I realize that I do not necessarily need a lot of friends. What I need are friends that are real, and are concerned about my wellbeing; friends who are solid and who will stand with me at all cost. I want friends who think well of me, while I think well of them. I want friends that will invest into our relationship. Life is too short to be spent on viral friends. What an accurate and valuable advice. Instead of having viral friends, it would be better to remain without friends.

Reconciling Friends

Sometime ago I tried to reconcile two friends. I cared deeply for both of them and was grieved that they were no longer friends. I was also in an awkward position because they both lived in the same city. When I approached the brother that was offended by the second brother, I found out that the emotional wounds were so deep and painful that he could not imagine being reconciled with the offending brother.

The average Christian would like to encourage or suggest a quick fix, but not every situation is that easy. When someone has been hurt deeply, then it might take him some time to heal. You cannot rash to such people and with a holier than thou attitude declare, "You are Christians and therefore should be reconciled immediately!" Some spiritual or emotional hurts do not have such an easy fix. As in our physical bodies, the deeper the cut the longer the time it takes to heal.

The brother in this story was terribly offended and eventually did accept the apology the other brother presented. However, even with the forgiveness he found it very hard to bring himself to the same place of trusting the other brother for future relationships. I visited both of them and encouraged each of them to continue seeking God for full recovery of their friendship.

I spent more time with the older brother that was offended, and encouraged him to seek ways and means of being fully reconciled. I prayed with him and then added the words, "You never know, this could be your future John Mark," referring to St. Paul's relationship with St. Mark which had so deteriorated at one point they could not serve together, yet later Paul asked Timothy to make sure he came with Mark to him and added, "for he is useful to me for ministry" (2 Timothy 4:11).

As in the story of Paul and Mark, we find that in life there are people that are harder to forgive than others. These are people that you have personally loved, supported, and sometimes even promoted in ministry or place of work, who then all at once turn around and attack you or betray you.

I vividly remember a time in our ministry when I was about to suggest the promotion of a particular person to a very prestigious position. I felt compelled that this person was the most qualified for that position. I even went ahead and shared this idea with some of the leaders in our organization. Then the worst happened! This individual turned against me and the leadership, viciously attacking everything we stood for. I was shocked because I had not expected this from this brother. The pain was greater because I had not seen it coming! However, later when I thought about the betrayal, I praised the Lord for this whole thing. It was much better that this person opposed us and fought us at that point than later when we would have promoted and established him in our ministry. The words of Paul became a reality to us. "All things work together for good to those who love God, to those who are the called according to *His* purpose" (Romans 8:28). This is exactly what happened. The Lord knew the heart of this brother and saved our ministry by having him leave that soon. God is faithful! It is not always good to complain when

> Sometimes even things we consider disappointments are our Father's expression of love and the care that He has for us and the ministries or processions.

some people leave or forsake you. Sometimes your life and ministry is far much better and enriched by their absence.

Sometimes even things we consider disappointments are our Father's expression of love and the care that He has for us and the ministries or professions He has called us into. When I complained to the Lord about the brother that was negative about our ministry, the Lord revealed to me, the greater benefit of not having to struggle with this brother later and in a situation which would cause more pain and sorrow to me and to the rest of the leadership. The Lord allowed me to be hurt and scandalized for a season, but for a better cause. I had to remind myself one more time that it is not about me, but about God's honor and glory. Our heavenly Father knows the best for us, our families, and the ministries He has entrusted to us.

I still remember hearing this beautiful, old song being sung by two outstanding saints when I was a young man in Primary school. Sister Helen Kariuki (then Helen Chege) and Sister Rahab Mwangi (then Rahab Kimani) sung this song when I was a teenager. They sung with such joy and passion, that it left a great impression and impact in my life. I still remember the chorus to this song:

> *God's way is best, I will not murmur,*
> *Although the end I may not see;*
> *Where'er He leads I'll meekly follow,*
> *God's way is best, is best for me*

(Charles W. Naylor, 1904 - Public domain)

I have thus learned over the years that God's way is not necessarily marked with smooth pathways, but that at times the road is rough and rocky, but His strong hand of righteousness is ever available for our support (See Isaiah 41:10). His way is always best even though we may not at times comprehend fully why He allows these things. We, however, know that all these things are for the good of His children.

Leaving Behind a Righteous Legacy

Just think about it, Joshua and Caleb did not feel really blessed when the nation of Israel picked up stones to kill them. I am sure none of them shouted "Halleluyah!" However, even though they were in such a dark valley in their lives, they were in the perfect will of God. God's way indeed is best even though sometimes it might lead through the darkest of valleys and at times through the hottest of deserts. His purpose is always connected to making us better instruments for the extension and promotion of His Kingdom and to His honor and glory.

> God's way indeed is best even though sometimes it might lead through the darkens of valleys and a times through the hottest of deserts.

When you look back at your life you will find periods or seasons when someone or some people hurt or injured you emotionally. Often times the enemy of our souls would have you to cling to your past. You continue holding those who hurt you in the bondage of un-forgiveness. The enemy uses this trick on almost all of us. He would have you to hold on to your sorrows and hurts. This is the one way the devil comes to steal, kill and destroy (John 10:10).

As long as you harbor un-forgiveness in your heart, you will walk in bondage. This bondage can sometimes deteriorate, and turn to bitterness and literally bring physical calamity to you. Many illness have their root in bitterness. "Research has compiled growing evidence that persons who bottle up their rage and remain unforgiving endanger their health" (Briggs, 34).

Brian Zahnd explains that the only way someone can face the future with hope is after allowing for the necessity of forgiveness in closing the door on a painful past. He observes that this is the only way that one can open the door to a promising future (Zahnd, 72).

Un-forgiveness leads to spiritual defeat. Why would anybody choose spiritual bondage, frustration, and pain over the joy that comes when two people are reconciled through forgiveness? Why would anybody want to invite physical maladies into their lives because of the sin of not forgiving others? All we need to do is allow the Holy Spirit to penetrate our inner beings and place in us the heart of Jesus. Jesus was hated and rejected by His own people; finally they placed Him on a cruel cross, but it was from that dreaded cross that he spoke some of the greatest words on forgiveness; "Father forgive them, for they do not know what they do (Luke 23:34)

Jesus went through the worst of betrayals. Not only was he rejected by His people, but his very own disciple betrayed Him. Then another disciple disowned him. He could have chosen bitterness, but He chose rather to forgive. The Lord calls us to walk in His footsteps. There is no greater lesson we can learn from our Master than learning to forgive those who have failed us or sinned against us.

Forgiveness releases you to come to a new level of receiving from the Father. Jesus taught us that if we did not forgiver others, then we should not expect our heavenly Father to forgive us (Matthew 6:14). This powerful, transformational power of forgiveness and unconditional love is what every child of God needs in their daily lives. Our brother Atwood reminds that experiencing and walking in such unconditional love and forgiveness is the only way the Kingdom of God can be expressed fully in our lives. "It is simply not enough to believe that He loves us. To be carried through life's anguish, we need something more. Not just the aroma of the banquet but the flavor, texture, and soporific excellence of it. And not just so we can endure. We need it so we can prosper in the Kingdom and proclaim and bring transformation!" (*Here and Coming*, 154-155).

Forgiveness releases you to come to a new level of receiving from the Father.

Forgiveness is a powerful key that unlocks all kinds of spiritual and physical breakthroughs. Have you been praying for some breakthroughs? Have you longed for great anointing in your life? The key may be in how you have walked in forgiveness or un-forgiveness. Search your soul and be honest to yourself; If there is even a little bit of un-forgiveness, then cry out to the Lord for mercy. You need to ask the Lord for the grace of forgiveness.

It really does not matter how much you are hurting. Someone might say, "You really do not know how much they hurt me." Or "You really do not know how so and so betrayed me." Indeed I may not know how much you were hurt, but one thing I know is that un-forgiveness, bitterness, and resentment have never and will never be a blessing to anybody. If anything these things will only cause spiritual defeat and frustration. The door way to your joy and freedom may rest in how you will allow the Holy Spirit to use you in forgiving that other person who has offended you.

Brian Zahnd says this about forgiveness, "The way of forgiveness does not forget the past, but through truth and reconciliation it finds a way beyond toxic memory" (*Unconditional*, 81). You may still remember the pain and sorrow that you experienced by those who hurt you, but there is still sufficient power, by God's enabling grace to forgive those who have hurt you.

In our Lord's prayer, we always pray, "Forgive us our sins even as we forgive those who trespass against us" (Matthew 6:12). May the Lord transform each of us by His grace and power so that we will indeed practice this prayer in our lives. When each of us practices forgiving each other, we will also experience peace and the joy unspeakable and full of glory (See 1 Peter 1:8). Only by God's grace and not our own power is this possible.

Armstrong Cheggeh

Lessons from Chapter 6

GOOD FRIENDS ARE a great asset. You cannot exchange them with anything. People who have no friends, or who are very poor in establishing friendships, and they end up living comparatively unhappy lives.

It is good to honor and please the people around you, but it is far better to please our heavenly Father.

God's friendship to us is unique in that He knows us in the best and deepest way there is to know anybody, and yet he loves us just as we are.

Friendships and lasting relationships call for sacrifice. You have to lose some things in order to gain the benefits of a good friendship. For your friendship to gain solidity, you will have to work towards unity and common values.

A friend is one whom you can completely be yourself with and never fear that he or she will judge you. A friend is someone that you can be open with and confide in with in complete trust.

Whatever our loving heavenly Father tells us to do is because His grace will always enable and empower us to obey.

Friends and counselors are important in our lives, but we should be very careful the friends we allow in our lives.

Any good friendship has to be ready for challenges, fights, and even disagreements. Being friends does not mean that you completely agree on everything. No one in the whole world would think or act exactly like the other.

Some spiritual or emotional hurts do not have an easy fix. As in our physical bodies, the deeper the cut the longer the time it takes to heal.

It is not always good to complain when some people leave or forsake you. Sometimes your life and ministry is far much better and enriched by their absence.

Sometimes even things we consider disappointments are our Father's expression of love and the care that He has for us and the ministries or professions He has called us into.

God's way is always best even though we many not at times comprehend fully why He allows some things in our lives.

We, however, know that all these things are for the good of His children.

As long as you harbor un-forgiveness in your heart, you will walk in bondage. This bondage can sometimes deteriorate, and turn to bitterness and literally bring physical calamity to you.

The Lord calls us to walk in His footsteps. There is no greater lesson we can learn from our Master than learning to forgive those who have failed us or sinned against us.

The door way to your joy and freedom may rest in how you will allow the Holy Spirit to use you in forgiving that other person who has offended you.

Chapter 7

God's Renewing Power

Strong For War

WHEN CALEB WENT to see Joshua about his inheritance, he made a very astounding statement, which seemed to be an exaggeration or an outright lie! He said, "As yet I am as strong this day as on the day that Moses sent me; just as my strength for war, both for going out and for coming in" (Joshua 14:11).

When you read these words you begin to wonder what this great man of God meant. How could he be as strong at age eighty-five as he was at age forty? There is no way, humanly speaking, that an eight-five-year-old man could be as strong as he was at age forty. Even the most godly or athletic of us loses physical strength and vigor as they get older, especially when the age difference is forty-five years.

The only thing I note is that Joshua and the rest of the Israelite leadership did not challenge Caleb and say, "What a liar or what an egocentric person you are!" They all seemed to agree with Caleb that he was actually as strong at age eighty-five as he was at forty. How could this be?

When I read this story I was reminded of one of the stories of David the king of Israel. There is no doubt that David was one of the mightiest of biblical warriors. Not only did he defeat and kill one of the most famous of the enemies of Israel by the name

Goliath, but he also fought many other battles and won most of them. However, when David got older, he was no longer as strong or swift as his younger days. Actually, during one battle he almost lost his life, were it not for the swiftness and strength of a younger Israelite soldier by the name Abishai the son of Zeruiah. Soon after this incident, the Israelite leadership decided not to have David go out for war. They just realized that he was too old to do the things he used to do as a younger warrior (2 Samuel 21:15-17).

I am bringing this story here to demonstrate an obvious fact; when a soldier gets older, however good he was when younger, he's no longer as swift or as strong as he was when younger, however spiritual he or she happens to be.

The question then is, "What did Caleb mean when he said, "I am as strong as on the day Moses sent me?" Even if the scriptures do not give any further explanation, I believe that what Caleb meant was more of what I would like to call, "a faith talk," or "the language of faith." It is the description that our brother Paul gives of the Christian walk, "For we walk by faith, not by sight" (2 Corinthians 5:7). It was not the physical strength of Caleb that would bring the victory, but more his walk of faith.

Caleb's walk with God for these many years had taught him great spiritual lessons. He had watched men who had seemed great in their own eyes and yet because of walking in the flesh, they had perished suddenly, especially the Canaanites they had conquered. This was also true of the ten other spies who had perished so suddenly after confessing their fear of being killed by the giants. Their confession became their reality. This should serve as a lesson and a warning for each of us. When we confess defeat and failures all the time, we often reap the fruit of our lips. There is power of death and life in our tongue (Proverbs 18:21).

Our brother Smith Wigglesworth says this of such confidence in God, "The righteousness that believes that every prayer uttered is going to bring the answer from God is better. There is a righteousness that is made known only to the heart that knows God. There is a side to the inner man that God can reveal only to the man who believes Him" (*Smith*, 81). The emphasis here is for the need for us to pray believing and trusting that God will respond to us in accordance to His word.

How often people fail in life for trusting in their strength and abilities. The scriptures admonish us to trust in the Lord with all of our hearts and not to lean upon our own understanding (Proverbs 3:5-6). Caleb had learned over these eighty-five years to see situations and circumstances in God's perspective, other than other people's perspectives or even his own.

Change of Language

We often come across situations and circumstances that are bigger than us or bigger than our abilities. When you walk with God and trust Him to see you through life's situations, you will eventually come to a place where even your language changes! When faced by a challenge that is bigger than you, you address it by faith, with the understanding that the battle has never been yours, but God's (2 Chronicles 20:16, 1 Samuel 17:47).

We believe in **Jehovah Sabaoth;** God of the heavenly armies! He has never lost a battle, and thus when facing a situation where you are about to possess the land, you can learn to walk and talk like Caleb. This means not having confidence in what you are or you can do, but more in who God is and what He has promised in His word. To do this you will need to be well versed with His word. The only way to be familiar with God's word is by studying and meditating on it regularly. I remember emphasizing this lesson in my first book in which I encouraged the believers to practice personal altar; setting a time and place for personal daily devotions (*Developing*, 140-141).

The Language of Faith

To the human ear when you speak like Caleb, it will seem as though you are confused or even lying. Indeed, how can you claim to have the ability to do the very things you could do when you were young? The answer to this question is, "In the faith language you are not only able to do what you could do in the past when you were young and strong, but you can now do even greater things because the ability to do those things does not depend on human strength, but on divine enablement. That is why Paul could say, "I can do all things through Christ who strengthens me (Philippians 4:13). When Christ is on your side, you are not only a conqueror, but "more than a conqueror!" (Romans 8:37).

There is no battle too big or too tough for those who have tasted the goodness of the Lord. David says that through God he could leap over a wall (Psalm 18:29). You note that he does not say, "By my own strength or wisdom I can leap over a wall." David knew that the power or secret of leaping over walls was found in his relationship with the Father. David also knew by experience that the only way he could face the mighty Goliath was by God's power. He had already faced a lion and bear by the same power (1 Samuel 17:36). He told Goliath, "You come to me with a sword, with a spear, and with a javelin, but I come to you in the name of the Lord of hosts the God of the armies of Israel, whom you have defied" (1 Samuel 17:45).

Our brother Daniel says, "…but the people who know their God shall be strong, and carry out great exploits." (Daniel 11:32). It is important to note how he combines the knowledge of God with the ability to do great exploits. He sees the knowledge of God as the enabling factor for believers to accomplish great things for the kingdom. The closer we get to our Father, the greater the ability to accomplish great things in the kingdom.

Our brother James puts it very well, "Draw near to God and He will draw near to you" (James 4:8). As we get closer to our heavenly Father, He in turn draws closer to us and thus we receive the power and anointing to accomplish those things we could not accomplish before. O that we would seek to know Him! Our brother Paul desired above all else to know Christ and the power of His resurrection (Philippians 3:10). His pursuit of God made him the great apostle he became.

Is there a task that you find too hard to accomplish right now? Have you been struggling in your Christian life or ministry for so long that you feel like giving up? What you need to do is, "Let go and let God." You need not struggle in your own strength. One old hymn says, "The arm of flesh will fail you; you dare not trust your own." Indeed the flesh will often fail us. Jonathan Lamb affirms these very words. "But the experience of all God's people is this: that the end of our resources is not the end of God's. It is at moments of pressure and weakness – sometimes at very extreme moments – that we are in the best position to prove God's grace and power" (*Integrity leading* 114). Often when we try to serve the Lord in own strength we end up in great disappointment.

Personally I have regretted many times when I tried to accomplish something in the flesh. I would fail so bad and sometimes hurt myself, my family or other people. Of course when I realized my own failures, sins, and foolishness, I would quickly come back to the Father in repentance and ask Him to lead me in the paths of righteousness. The forgiveness and healing would come, but then I had already wasted time and lost great opportunities. It always pays to consult with our heavenly Father before we begin any project or enter into any ministry. In most instances your failures and sin do not only affect your life individually; it affects others around you. Thus there is need to seek God every step of the way.

The Knowledge of God

Our intimacy and knowledge of God will definitely affect what we become and what kind of service we render to our heavenly Father. Caleb's knowledge of God and his friendship with God did not begin in the land of promise. It began in the wilderness. He was a friend of God all through the very rough years of the wilderness wanderings. Some of us want to wait until things and circumstances are better in our lives before we can follow the Lord whole-heartedly. Not so for Caleb. He loved and served the Lord even in the roughest of the storms and in the darkest of hours. Blackaby and King remind us of the need to wait upon the Lord, all through life and that it takes time to be prepared for great roles in God's kingdom. "Don't get in a hurry. God may spend years preparing your character or developing your love relationship with Him. Don't be discouraged if the assignment or "call" does not come immediately" (<u>Experiencing God</u>, 116).

Over all these years, God was still preparing Caleb for the great service ahead of him. It seems that God has some wilderness wandering for each of His generals, even though each wilderness season is different from one servant to the other. May the Lord give us the grace to endure and stand firm even in times of the wilderness. These wilderness seasons do not last forever. The Bible tells us that God's favor is for life, but that weeping may endure for a night, but joy *comes* in the morning (Psalm 30:5).

> It seems that God has some wilderness wandering for each of His generals, even though each wilderness season is different from one servant to the to the other.

When God declared that Caleb would definitely make it to the land of promise and that his descendants would benefit from his faithfulness, he was still in the wilderness. May God help us to trust Him even while going through the wilderness experiences. Do not wait for a better season before you can trust God or serve Him in whatever capacity He has called you to serve. You can honor Him, and even praise Him in the wilderness.

What are you going through right now? Are you in some wilderness experiences? May the Lord help you to have a Caleb-like attitude. Just worship and bless the Name of the Lord in the wilderness. Speak the language of faith. "Faith is the substance of things hoped for, the evidence of things not seen (Hebrews 11:1). You can still speak the language of faith even though you cannot see much right now. We walk by faith not by sight (2 Corinthians 5:7). Things and circumstances around you may change from time to time, but our faith in God should remain constant and ever growing like that of Caleb. This is why he could say, "As yet, I am as strong this day as on the day that Moses sent me; just as my strength was then, so now is my strength for war, both for going out and for coming in" (Joshua 14:11).

Give me this Mountain!

At age eighty-five Caleb visited his old friend Joshua, accompanied by other leaders from the tribe of Judah (Joshua 14: 6). As a veteran soldier, that was also greatly admired, liked, and respected in the whole nation of Israel, he could have asked for any portion of the conquered territories in Canaan. God, Himself had declared on two occasions that Caleb was a very special person. When God declares somebody to be special and faithful to Him, nobody can doubt or questions it. However, even with such a wonderful commendation from God Himself, Caleb still asked for some unconquered territory! He did not ask for a life of ease. He asked to conquer the unclaimed land.

Caleb did not ask for the land that the other Israelites had settled in, as though to demonstrate how great and powerful he was. His story reminds us of the transition that took place in most places in Africa when the African nations got their independence from the European colonial powers. Most of the African leaders quickly grabbed the best of the land for themselves and for their children! This was not so for Caleb. Caleb allowed almost everybody in Israel to settle on their land before claiming his inheritance. He then probably surprised many by asking for the unconquered territory, but not only unconquered, but also the most dangerous of the unconquered territories of the enemy.

Why on earth would Caleb ask for the challenging unconquered territory which was still in the hands of their enemies? What does an eighty-five-year-old man mean by asking for unconquered territory? Wouldn't he rather ask for the conquered land. Not so for this man of faith! He had walked long enough with God to know that in God's mind, the conquered and the unconquered are the same! God had already declared the victory of the Israelites even before they settled in the land. God had already declared to the nation of Israel, "Every place that the soles of your feet will tread upon I have given you, as I said to Moses" (Joshua 1:3). The nation was forty-five years late in claiming that which already belonged to them.

Therefore, in Caleb's mind the new territory was already conquered because he would not do it in his own strength, but in God's strength. He based his stand on the promises of God. There is no problem bigger than God's promise. What God has promised He will fulfill in spite of the challenges ahead. Later on we find Joshua affirming this very idea in Joshua 21:45, "Not a word failed of any good thing which the Lord had spoken to the house of Israel. All came to pass."

A Life full of Passion

Most of us after having served the Lord for a while lose the excitement and passion we used to have when we first came to Christ. We begin to falter and sometimes take God's word for granted. We get to a place in our lives where we are no longer as excited about the things of God and His promises. We become "too familiar" with the things of God. For Caleb, it seems that the older he got the more daring he became! His passion and love for God grew with the passing of years. It seems that at age eighty-five he remembered all of God's promises to him and he did not want to die without accomplishing everything in the assignment that the Lord had given him. Calvin Miller says that there is nothing as bad as lacking passion while serving the Lord. "No Christian is quite so dead as one whose vitality has been sapped by being out of touch with God" (Into the Depths, 30). What a joy on the other hand for someone to keep serving the Lord with passion even to their eighties like Caleb.

One of the assignments given to Caleb was to possess the unconquered territory of the giants. It seems that most of the other Israelites had all along been afraid of tackling this territory. I guess the words of the ten spies had great impact upon them in that for all these forty-five years nobody had dared venture in the giants' territory. Caleb dared believe God for the worst territory.

Has your walk with the Lord slackened as the years passed? If you lack passion and excitement in your life, just ask the Lord to forgiven you and also fill you with His love (Romans 5:5). That way you will touch others not in your strength, but in Christ's love and power. Passion grows out of a closer walk with the Master. God called the church at Ephesus to a closer walk with Him (Revelation 2:4). This church was not walking in worldliness as the church of Laodicea, but they needed to rekindle their passion for Christ. As we gain our passion for Christ and His kingdom, nothing will be too big a challenge. We, too, can face any of the giants in our lives as we come to a realization that when God is on our side nothing shall be impossible (Matthew 17:20, 19:26, Romans 8:31).

The Habitation of the Giants

It is interesting to note the area Caleb asked for. It was not only part of the unconquered territory, but also the land of the giants! Remember what the other ten spies had said, "There we saw the giants (the descendants of Anak came from the giants); and we were like grasshoppers in our own sight and so we were in their sight" (Numbers 13:33).

It seems like all these years Caleb did not allow himself to forget those words. In his quiet moments he recalled the words of those cowardly spies, "We were like grasshoppers." Caleb's mind could not rest. I don't know why he waited so long, but in his mind he would always answer, "No way, I am nobody's grasshopper!" I am a child of the Most High God." He made this confession for so long, that finally he had to act upon his faith. At age eighty-five he asked for the land of the giants. He said, "It may be that the Lord will be with me, and I shall be able to drive them out as the Lord said" (Joshua 14:12).

Joshua 14:15 says that Hebron previous name was Kirjath Arba, and goes on to explain that Arba was the greatest man among the Anakim. In other words, Caleb was conquering and inheriting the land of the greatest of the giants that ever lived!

When he received Hebron as an unconquered territory, he moved in and literally drove the three sons of Anak from the land (Joshua 15:14). Isn't it interesting that the very giants that the ten spies feared were the same people that Caleb conquered, drove out, and dwelt in their land. It was this same land, as we shall see later, that became the inheritance of Caleb's children just as the Lord had said. His blessing and inheritance was not only for his own lifetime, but would continue to be a blessing to his future generations just as the Lord had promised him.

Your Unconquered Territory

My prayer is that as you read this chapter faith will well up within your heart for any unconquered territory in your life. If God could give such a great victory to an eighty-five-year old man who dared believe in His promises, He surely will remember you if you take Him at His word and stand on His promises. All you need is faith in God. Believe His word. Believe that what God has done for any other saint in His word or in church history, He will do for you. This reminds me of that old song, "It's no secret what God can do, what He's done for others, He will do for you (Public domain, Stuart Hamblen, 1951).

Remember this: "God does not show partiality" (Acts 10:38). He does not, and will never discriminate. You are a child of His love. What is it that He had placed in your mind? What visions and dreams has he placed in your heart? You do not need to wait until you are eighty-fives to receive your inheritance. Rise up by faith and possess your inheritance! There is no promise too big or too precious for any of His children. The scriptures tell us that every good and perfect gift comes from our heavenly Father (James 1:17).

Lessons from Chapter 7

THE CLOSER WE get to our Father, the greater the ability to accomplish great things in the kingdom.

In most instances your failures and sin do not only affect your life individually; it affects others around you. Thus there is need to seek God every step of the way.

Our intimacy and knowledge of God will definitely affect what we become and what kind of service we render to our heavenly Father.

It seems that God has some wilderness wandering for each of His generals, even though each wilderness season is different from one servant to the other.

Do not wait for a better season before you can trust God or serve Him in whatever capacity He has called you to serve. You can honor Him, and even praise Him in the wilderness.

There is no problem bigger than God's promise. What God has promised He will fulfill in spite of the challenges ahead.

You are a child of God's love. What is it that He had placed in your mind? What visions and dreams has He placed in your heart? You do not need to wait until you are eighty-fives to receive your inheritance. Rise up by faith and possess your inheritance!

There is no promise too big or too precious for any of His children.

Armstrong Cheggeh

Chapter 8

Children: A Blessed Heritage

GOD PROMISED CALEB the son of Jephunneh that the blessing he would receive in the land of promise would not only be his, but also for his future generations (Numbers 14:24). This promise, of course meant that the Lord would definitely bless him with children who will benefit from their father's constancy and faithfulness.

Even though we do not know much about Caleb's family, at least we know that he had a daughter by the name Achsah.

Achsah came to her father as she had already married her cousin Othniel and asked her father for some extra land. Those days it was acceptable even for first cousins to get married. "So she dismounted from her donkey and Caleb said to her, 'what do you wish?' She answered, 'Give me a blessing. Since you have given me land in the south, give me also springs of water." So he gave her the upper springs and the lower springs (Joshua 15:18b -19).

One thing I note in this episode is that there were no struggles between the father and the daughter. There was such a freedom on the part of Achsah in that she did not hesitate to ask for the special blessing from her father. The father on the other hand seems to have been waiting for this request. He granted her this request immediately.

Respect for both Husband and Father

In this short episode you will note two very important things. Achsah loved and respected both her father and her new husband, Othniel. Even though she was newly married, she did not ignore her husband and approach her father for land without her husband's blessing. She discussed the issue with her husband first, before presenting it to her father.

Women in the church would do well to practice honoring those two important men in their lives; your father and your husband. Your father will always be your father, whether he is good or not. Sometimes you may not like all that he represents for indeed there are parents who may not deserve a lot of respect because of their attitudes or their lifestyles. However, even though your parents have acted in ways that hurt you or were simply unfair and unjust, always remember this you cannot win their lives with hatred and strive. Love covers a multitude of sins (1 Peter 4:8). Pray that the Lord, by His Holy Spirit will help you to love your parents just the way they are and not necessarily the way they should be. Since the bible commands us to love our enemies, then how much more our very own parents, even when they are not just, loving or fair.

The point in this story though is that Achsah was raised in a family that taught her the value of loving and respecting both her father and her husband. Her father's influence in her life did not discourage her from pursuing her dreams and vision, but rather encouraged her to seek out the best for herself and her family. Pastor John Hagee reminds us of the power and influence of a father to both his wife and children. "The Father is the spiritual authority. Father, what you say to your wife or children literally predestines their intellectual, emotional, and perhaps even their physical development" (*Day of Deception*, 131).

Ron Rand tells of a study which revealed that when both parents attend church regularly seventy-two per cent of their children continue in the faith. If only the mother attends, then only fifteen per cent of the children remain in church, but when the father attend regularly, 55 per cent of the children remain faithful (*For Fathers,* 82-83). How important then for fathers to be involved in the lives of their children, especially in the growing years.

Confidence Gained from Up-Bringing

Being a wise woman, Achsah knew that in time she would most likely have children who would need land. She knew the value of land. Since she was better informed on what belonged to the family, she advised her husband on what he should request from her father (Joshua 15:18). Apparently Othniel did not act fast enough and therefore Achsah goes on and makes the request.

The point I am making here is that Achsah, unlike what many people think of Old Testament women, was not timid. She was not only free with both her husband and father, but had such confidence in talking to both of them, even on matters of land. What other subject would be more important, than that of land, especially at this particular time in the history of the nation of Israel. If people are settling up in a new country, the most important asset is land. If Achsah could discuss matters of land, then she definitely could discuss any other subject with both her father and her husband.

The question then is, "Where did achsah get such confidence?" The answer is obvious. She was raised in a good family that encouraged even the girls in the family to know their rights and privileges as children of God and members of their individual families. She was raised in a family where children were encouraged to think and make important decisions by themselves. Myles Munroe called this "passing of the baton," an obligation on the part of those in leadership, and in this case on the part of the parents. "The greatest obligation of true leadership is to transfer the deposit of knowledge, wealth, experience, influence, relationships, and understanding to the next generation" (*Passing it On,* 3).

Claiming the Right Things

Caleb's children were raised to know what really mattered in life. Land was the most important and valued asset in Israel. When Caleb's children set their goals and plans they knew exactly what to prioritize. How many newly married Israelite wives were talking of owning land and springs of water? Well, in Caleb's family children knew exactly what to ask for and the things that really mattered in order to establish a family. They most likely also knew of God's promise to their father, "But my servant Caleb, because he has a different spirit in him and has followed me fully, I will bring into the land where he went and his descendants shall inherit it" (Numbers 14:24).

How have you raised your children? Do they have the right values? If and when the opportunity presented itself, would they have responded like Achsah? Would they have claimed the same promise that God had promised to the family? It is interesting to note that the Lord promised land to Caleb. His children asked for the very thing the Lord had promised. They had learned their lessons well.

In a previous chapter I explained that it is not important just to learn to, "name and claim things." The important thing is to love God with all your heart, and then to know what He has promised and the conditions attached to these promises.

There is not one promise in the scriptures that does not have some conditions to be fulfilled by those who claim that promise. Another important thing to remember is that there is no promise too good or sacred for any of His children. Each of His children qualifies to receive His many and precious promises. "His divine power has given to us all things that pertain to life and godliness, thorough the knowledge of Him who called us by glory and virtue" (1 Peter 1:3). God is faithful. All of God's promises in Christ are "yes and in Him Amen" (2 Corinthians 1:20). His promises are true. He will fulfill all the promises He has made to His children.

The bible says, "If you then, being evil, know how to give

good gifts to your children, how much more will your Father who is in heaven give good things to those who ask Him" (Matthew 7:11). Therefore, there is no question as to whether God would fulfill His promises. He will fulfill His promises, but we have to come to Him on His own terms and not on our own. When we get intimate with Him and know His way, we will also know how best to approach Him. Like Achsah we will receive that which we will have petitioned for because it will be based on what He has promised to His children.

The Prayer that Gets Answered

What brought such a swift answer to Achsah was not only in the way she approached her father, but also because she knew the details of the family property. She knew where the upper and lower springs were and whom they belonged to. She could not ask for promises that were not covered by the promises of her father. You, too, need to know your Father intimately and develop a closer relationship with Him. This relationship will also bring you to a better comprehension of the "family's property." You will know what to ask for when the opportune time comes.

Our heavenly Father is far wealthier than Caleb. He owns the cattle on a thousand hills (Psalm 50:10). Silver and gold are His (Haggai 2:8), and the whole world and all its fullness is His (Psalm 50:12b). There is nothing in this world that is too dear or too precious for any of God's children. Paul says, "He who did not spare His own Son, but delivered Him up for us all, how shall He not with Him also freely gives us all things (Romans 8:32). If He did not spare His very own Son but delivered Him for us, then it means that all His heavenly treasures are all available to His children, for nothing can compare to the gift of His son.

Therefore, if and when any of us prays and make some petitions or supplications, if we don't see the answer, we need to ask ourselves several things. First, we have to know that there are times that the Lord chooses not to answer immediately even when we pray for the right things. Right things do not mean right seasons. There are times that you will pray for something really good, but the Lord in His excellent greatness and unfathomable wisdom knows the very depths of our souls. He knows us much better than we know ourselves. He may want you to wait for a while and mature some more before he can entrust you with particular ministries or gifts.

Another important aspect to consider as we make petitions is the purpose for which we are asking for that particular thing. Will that petition or supplication bring glory to the Lord and will it build His Kingdom? Remember this, The Kingdom of God revolves around God's will and purpose. It does not matter how sincere and how intensive we pray if our petitions and supplications are not in support of kingdom businesses.

> Remember this, The Kingdom of God revolves around God's will and purpose.

Openness to Children

As noted above we see a great openness between a father and daughter in the story of Caleb and Achsah his daughter. Such openness and freedom in a family is a very important element in the relationship between parents and children. Children need to feel free to share whatever is in their hearts with their parents. If your children find it hard to discuss their personal issues or the challenges they are going through then your relationship needs attention. You may need to improve on your attitude and communication skills.

Over the years, by God's marvelous grace I've learned of the need to open up to my children. I've cultivated a deep relationship with each of my five children in that they will usually come to me, even now that they are adults, and talk to me about any subject or challenge that they are facing. Even as of today, anytime one of my grown children calls on a particular issue, I get to thank God because it is an indication of the freedom they gained as they grew up in our home.

Let your children be free with you and ask you whatever questions they have. If you are not available to them then someone else will. Their friends or other people will be available to them and may give them the answers you would not have approved or appreciated. Always remember that these children will not always be young. The time you spend with those children is not wasted. Your words of wisdom shared in times of family altar and your quality time spent with any of your children becomes a seed for the future of your children.

Comparing the priorities we give to our jobs as compared to the priority we give to our children, Ron Rand says, "Believe me, there is not a client more important or deserving of your time than your child. Your client could go to another business man to get his work done, but there is no other man your child can turn to for a father's love" (*For Fathers*, 80-81).

Now, you have to know a little bit of my life to understand what a transformation this was – accepting the idea that parents could be open and freely share with their children. I was raised in Central Kenya in a Kikuyu family. In my generation, children rarely asked questions to the adult. Actually, when guests came to the house, the children were sent out of the house, or were made to keep quiet the whole time the guests were around. They were there to be seen, but not to be heard.

Fathers were especially distanced from their children. Basically being playful or joking with a father was unheard of. To this day many African fathers will not allow any form of playfulness with their children. These African men would consider it almost anathema to go play ball or swim with their sons. Of course life is changing fast and attitudes are changing and that for the better. In recent years we find few African fathers who take their families for vacations and even allow for some playfulness and more sharing and close communication between them and their children. I pray that more fathers from such cultures will see the need for this closeness as time goes on.

One true story illustrates this best. One young lady was frustrated because her father was not available to her. Very soon in her pursuit of love and appreciation she got pregnant by a man who also refused to marry her. Soon her father's insults and oppression were unbearable for her. She opted to take her son away from home and went and took the job she had never dreamed of taking. She became a bar maid. However, since she had always been a very fine person, everybody could not believe how well behaved this bar maid was!

One of those who noticed her was an older man whose wife had left him. He noticed how this lovely girl behaved. She did not behave like the rest of the bar maids. He observed her from a far, and then eventually developed a great liking for this girl. To make the long story short, they soon fell in love and got married. This precious girl became one of the best women in that village. I knew her personally and nobody would have believed that she had formerly been a bar maid.

This teaches us two things: first what a father or mother says or does to a child can alter them for life, sometimes for better and at other times for worse. The words of the father in this story drove her daughter to be a bar maid. What you say to your sons and daughters can make or destroy them. Words have power. The bible says, "Death and life are in the power of the tongue" (Proverbs 18:21a). You can give life or death to your family by what you say.

Do not Provoke your Children to Wrath

The bible cautions the fathers not to provoke their children to anger (Ephesians 6:4). When you treat your children negatively, you plant a seed of negativity and anger into their spirit. Interview lots of people in prison and one of the main reasons they are in that prison is the kind of home they grew up in. According to Quinsey et al. "Most researchers have observed that the social context of the family plays a critical role in the unfolding of juvenile delinquency (80) and that, "the effective quality of the parent–child relationship is crucial in the development of antisocial behavior" (Quinsey, 85). A child that is surrounded by love, concern, and care will most likely not be involved in crime.

Nick Cuthbert cautions parents on the seeds that they sow in the lives of the children. He says that if one sowed negative things into the lives of the child, "...you will end yours days with a great deal of regret as those closest to you are damaged by the pain you have caused" (*How to*, 65).

Parent better be warned of the words they say to their children. Be careful of saying things like, "You good for nothing." "You will amount to nothing." These negative words that some people say to their children become almost curses to them. Some of these children grow to be exactly those things you declared over their lives. Practice honor and respect for your Children, and an openness to discuss issues with them and you will be surprised as to how open and close your children will be to you.

Calling for Change and Balance

I have lived in Africa and also in the Western world and sometimes I have longed to see a balance between the two worlds. I see hardness and an almost unyielding obstinacy on the part of the African parents, especially the fathers. As I said before, most of these fathers feel as though being close and interacting with their children and allowing for playfulness or open discussion will lowers their dignity as men. They feel as though such an attitude will lower their standing in the community.

On the other hand I see a freedom that goes beyond the acceptable biblical honor for parents in the Western world. In America, generally speaking, most children are raised to see their fathers more as they would see their friends and age mates. The concept of honor for fathers is lacking so much in the Western world, especially in America. The playfulness goes beyond the father-son to more of boy-boy playfulness. I see a melting down of the virtue of honor for parents, especially the male parent. This is worse in the African American communities.

Begin "Cultivation" Early

It is hard for the honor and respect for parents to begin late in life. It has to begin early. If both parents teach the child honor when he or she is still a toddler, then most likely that child will show honor when they grow up. The scripture teaches us to, "train up a child in the way he should go (Proverbs 22:6). You cannot leave your children on their own and hope that all will be well. Every godly parent should take up the responsibility of taking care of his or her children. Be sure you know your children closely. Watch their steps and know their friends.

Several years back when our children were still home my wife and I decided to be inviting all our children's friends to our house whenever we had a special occasion like birthdays or other get-togethers. The idea here was not only so our children could come and enjoy a good time with their friends, but also so that we could become familiar with the children that our children associated with. This is an aspect that we would recommend to other parents. Get to know the people that are closest to your children. Children influence each other, and so it becomes very important to know your children's friends and their backgrounds.

Make time for the Children

I really like the story of Caleb and his daughter. In Caleb you see a man who had real and genuine interest in his family. Even though we know him as a senior leader in Israel, and more in the tribe of Judah, he did not forsake his family in order to serve the nation. He had time both for his political and national role and also for his family. However busy we get, we need to make time for our families. Those children grow fast. I can still remember when mine were just toddlers. Now my youngest child is twenty-one and has just gone to college. We have now begun the empty nesters chapter of our life.

Every parent needs to be loving, caring, and available to your children whenever they can. Those quality moments spent with your children are so valuable. You will never regret that you spent quality time with your children. Actually the opposite is true. Most older people have almost always wished they had spent more time with their children. They often wish they had taken some vacations and gone out with their families. I know I spent time with my family, but I've also wished I had spent more time with the children as they grew up.

Spanking "Spare not the Rod"

The Scriptures in many instances have endorsed spanking as a method of discipline (Proverbs 22:15, 23:13-14). Of course most of the modern day teaching and secular psychologists would oppose this method. To them any method that brings physical pain to a child will definitely alter and damage their emotions. What a lie! If that were the case almost all of the Africans of my generation would have been emotionally damaged, and yet my generation has become the builder generation both in the African church and Africa nations in general. I can say with all confidence that spanking given with fairness, and firmness, is one of the best and most effective ways of disciplining the younger children. Children have not changed from the days of Solomon, and of course the biblical standards have not changed either.

Spanking should be reserved only for serious offenses. For example when a child tells a lie or acts in open disobedience, especially on the already laid out rule of the particular family, then he or she invites the spanking. What I mean by already laid out rules, is that the parents are wholly responsible to lay down the rules and instruct the children on right behavior. As a loving, caring, responsible parent you should never, ever punish or disciple a child for something you never instructed or talked to them about.

When my children were younger, we would sometimes spend time during our family altar time to discuss the "rules of the family." I wanted my children to fully understand our family standards. They had the right to know who they are and what our family stood for. We discussed these issues with the children so much so, that each child knew what exactly was expected of them and how to act when confronted by a particular challenge or temptation. If then, they failed after the discussion and explanations, then I also felt it my responsibility to discipline because they already knew how they should have behaved.

Of course when the bible talks of the rod, it does not necessary mean a "fighting or defense rod" as must have been used by shepherds to defend the sheep from wild animals. The rod should not be a large and heavy stick which can cause damage to your child's body. You are not to use the rod of correction to your children as though fighting an enemy. Actually you should never use the rod of correction when you are very angry. You should always give yourself time to "cool off" before you apply the rod, especially if the disobedience brought great anger. You are not disciplining your child as though to destroy and damage their body or emotion. . Discipline should always be a corrective measure and for the betterment of the children.

Even in saying this, I have to admit that there are other non-spanking forms of discipline, especially when the children get a little bigger and older. However, the scripture seems to show that nothing drives out rebellion, and false ways in a child, like spanking (Proverbs 13:24, 19:18, 22:15, 23:13, 23:14, 29:15). Actually these verses say that a child so corrected will not die, but rather will gain wisdom. Indeed a child that is spanked in the right way will learn quickly to honor parental authority. When the bible says that a child thus spanked will not die, points to the same point I made earlier that in spanking you are not trying to destroy or damage your child's body, but rather to teach him or her, the foolishness of his or her behavior.

Restricted Privileges

This kind of discipline is when a privilege of going somewhere or being involved in a certain activity is deprived to a child because of bad or unacceptable behavior. This can involve denying a child from being involved in a certain sport for a while, limiting of restricting the viewing of television for a while, being with certain friends for a while. It can also involve removing driving privileges to a child for a season. As a parent you need to calculate what restriction has the greater impact or consequences. It is always proper to use a restriction that will be felt by the child and something that will make the particular child avoid the particular activity that would attract the same response from the parents.

The restriction or removal of privileges will only be effective if the child will definitely miss the activity that is being denied. If there is no pain or anguish of the denied privilege, then the disciplinary measure has not worked. The measure only works if the child feels some form of mental pain or anguish in that, that particular activity or thing has been denied. For example, if a parent denies a child the use of the cell phone so that for a while he or she is not able to communicate with some particular peer group, it will definitely affect the child in a way that they will want not to offend again.

Withdrawal and Expulsion

Another effective way to discipline a child is getting them away by themselves. By being sent into their rooms by themselves, the child is taught the purpose and joy of being with other people. In their room for two or so hours, they feel bored and lonely. They get a chance to be by themselves and understand the value of interconnectedness and fellowship. Next time they are tempted to do what prompted their parents to send them out into their rooms alone, they will most likely think twice about what to do.

Rebellion by older children, especially after high school days, may mean actual expulsion from home. This means a complete separation for a season with the rest of the children. This kind of discipline may be applied if the child has done something that will definitely affect the younger children. For example if this grown child keeps on challenging the authority of the parents, or being rude to the parents, such a behavior can definitely affect how the other children will respond in the future. Such a child should be sent out of the home to learn his lessons out of the home. As a parent you cannot keep on feeding and paying bills for a child that is also rebellious. Let him go into the world and be taught by the world how to behave. A Swahili saying goes, "He who refuses to listen to his mother will definitely be taught by the world."

Of course there are situations that as a responsible parent you may still feel responsible for a rebellious child, especially in case of drug abuse. You might be angry about the behavior, but still make plans for the child to go to a rehabilitation center. That way you will have gotten him out of your house, but will still be doing something to help him change his ways. If, for example you suggest that he goes to the rehabilitation center and he refuses, then definitely feel free, and without guilt send him out of your home.

Praise Your Children

One of the most important things to remember when raising children is to praise them when they have done that which is right and responsible. You raise them to know and understand that you do not only see the negative things in their lives. Children are overly pleased when praised by their parents. It becomes an incentive to behave in a better way. If your children note that you only criticize them for bad behavior and never praise them when they have performed well, then you create in them a spirit of low esteem and failure. By praising and encouraging children, Parents can greatly strengthen their self-esteem.

Concern for future Generations

There is an interesting story in the book of 2 Kings. King Hezekiah showed all his wealth to the emissaries that had been sent by king of Babylon by the name Berodach-Baladan, when they came to comfort him after he had been sick. Isaiah the prophet rebuked him for his act and also prophesied doom to his family. The prophet said that the king's sons and indeed his whole family would go into captivity and even serve as Eunuchs in Babylon. Instead of being sorrowful and repenting, he rejoiced in that those evil things would take place after his death! (See 2 Kings 20:19). To this man, it did not matter what happened to his family as long as he himself did not suffer. What a foolish attitude!

Hezekiah's attitude was quite selfish. None of us ought to live for just ourselves. We should be concerned of the future of our families, our churches, and our nations. What you do today will definitely affect future generations either negatively or positively. We should impact and invest in our children, our families, our churches, and nations, so that their lives will even be better than those of our own generation. We should pray and speak a better future for our future generations.

Dr. Myles Munroe emphasized the need for leaders, and in this matter the parents to consider the impact they have on those they leave behind. "No matter how much you may learn, achieve, accumulate, or accomplish, if it all dies with you, then you are a generational failure. The act and art of mentoring are the manifestations of the highest level of maturity and self-confidence" (*Passing it On*, ix). The question here then is what kind of impact or legacy did you leave for your children? Have you passed on the legacy of love, godliness, and integrity to your children?

Armstrong Cheggeh

Lessons from Chapter 8

EVEN THOUGH YOUR parents have acted in ways that hurt you or were simply unfair and unjust, always remember that you cannot win their lives with hatred and strive.

There is not one promise in the scriptures that does not have some conditions to be fulfilled by those who claim that promise.

You, too, need to know your Father intimately and develop a closer relationship with Him. This relationship will also bring you to a better comprehension of the "family's property." You will know what to ask for when the opportune time comes.

The Kingdom of God revolves around God's will and purpose. It does not matter how sincere and how intensive we pray if our petitions and supplications are not in line with His will and purpose and in support of kingdom businesses.

If your children find it hard to discuss their personal issues or the challenges they are going through then your relationship needs attention. You may need to improve on your attitudes and communication skills.

What you say to your sons and daughters can make or destroy them. Words have power. The bible says, "Death and life are in the power of the tongue" (Proverbs 18:21a). You can give life or death to your family by what you say.

When you treat your children negatively, you plant a seed of negativity and anger into their spirit.

You will never regret that you spent quality time with your children. Actually the opposite is true. Many older people have almost always wished they had spent more time with their children.

Spanking should be reserved only for serious offenses. For example when a child tells a lie or acts in open disobedience, especially on the already laid out rule of the particular family, then he or she invites the spanking.

You are not to use the rod of correction to your children as though fighting an enemy. You should never use the rod of correction when you are very angry.

Another effective way to discipline a child is getting them away by themselves. By being sent into their rooms by themselves, the child is taught the purpose and joy of being with other people.

There are situations that as a responsible parent you may still feel responsible for a rebellious child, especially in case of drug abuse. You might be angry about the behavior, but still make plans for the child to go to a rehabilitation center.

One of the most important things to remember when raising children is to praise them when they have done that which is right and responsible. You raise them to know and understand that you do not only see the negative things in their lives.

We should impact and invest in our children, our families, our churches, and nations, so that their lives will even be better than those of our own generation.

Chapter 9

Raise up the Foundation for many Generations (Part 1)

> *"Those from among you shall build the old waste places; you shall raise up the foundations of many generations; and you shall be called the repairer of the breach, the restorer of streets to dwell in"*
> *(Isaiah 58:12).*

ABOUT FIVE YEARS AGO, I received a phone call from a very close family and ministry friend, who has since gone to be with the Lord. Rev. Shirley Brown was my one of my students, about thirty years ago at the Greater Works School of ministry in Monroeville, Pennsylvania. After her bible school training the Lord entrusted her with a powerful ministry called the Victorious Faith Evangelistic Outreach. Over the years I have been invited to speak in their lovely church or when they have had special occasions. This time she called me when Covenant Theological Seminary decided to honor her by conferring on her an honorary Doctor of Ministry degree. She asked me to be one of the two main speakers that would speak on that auspicious occasion.

I was glad that I would be taking part in this occasion that was honoring a very close friend. I gladly accepted to be one of the speakers. After a short time she called again to make a very unusual request. For almost thirty years she had never given me the topic or chapter from which I should speak, but for this occasion she did. She called to ask if I could consider preaching from either John chapter fifteen or Isaiah chapter fifty-eight, the two chapters that many of the Lord's servants had identified as a definition of her ministry.

Of course I knew what chapter I would choose – John fifteen! Who would find it hard to preach on Jesus as the true vine and believers as the branches? I think every preacher has preached from this chapter. However, there was a problem; she told me that whatever book I chose then the other preacher would have to speak from the other book.

I thought for a while, and it did not take me long to know what the Lord would have me to do. It would be very selfish of me, a seasoned minister of the Word to quickly choose to speak from the easier chapter. I called Rev. Brown and said, "Let the other preacher choose the chapter he wants first. If he chooses the chapter in John then I will preach from Isaiah." The other preacher chose John fifteen, which meant I now had to preach from Isaiah fifty-eight.

Every time I had preached from Isaiah fifty-eight, I emphasized the subject of prayer and fasting. I would preach on, "God's chosen fast," or "The right attitude in prayer and fasting, or just, "How to fast." So, it was interesting when I opened my bible to read this chapter one more time. I was wondering, "What has a chapter about prayer and fasting got to do with a day when someone is being conferred with a doctoral degree?" Of course prayer and fasting are foundational topics; any spiritual leader has to have seasons of prayer and fasting in their lives. However, I did not think I should preach on prayer and fasting on this particular occasion. As I opened the bible and began reading, I found out that I was in for a big surprise! This chapter contained much more than prayer and fasting.

God's Word deeper than our finite Minds

I have been greatly blessed and at the same surprised at how deep the word of God is. Over these forty-six years – yes, it's been forty-six years since I received Jesus into my heart. I got saved in the East African Revival movement, which literally touched thousands of lives all over the East Africa region. Over these years I have come to know that the Word of God is far deeper than our little finite minds can fathom. God has declared in His word that His thoughts and His ways are much higher than our ways and our thoughts (Isaiah 55:8-9). I have come to believe in this word much more now than when I first believed.

It takes the Spirit of God to move over our minds and spirits for each of us to comprehend the depth of the riches in His word. I am saying all this to make a very important and profound statement: No one ever gained a full and perfect knowledge of God and His will while here on earth. This is why faith is so important to a believer. There are scores of things in the Word that you may never know fully, but you just accept them by faith. The scripture says that without faith, it is impossible to please God (Hebrews 11:6). We will continue to learn and grow until the time when we shall know just as we are known, when we shall be like Him, for we shall see Him as He is (1 Corinthians 13:12, 1 John 3:2). O how I love and long for His appearing!

Isaiah Chapter Fifty-Eight

When I began to read Isaiah fifty-eight in preparation for the big day, I learned something that I had not learned before even after having been saved for forty-six years, and that is why I mentioned how deep God's word is. As stated previously, whenever I preached on Isaiah fifty-eight, it was always about fasting. Now as I read it one more time, one verse caught my attention. "Those from among you shall build the old waste places; you shall raise up the foundations of many generations; and you shall be called the repairer of the breach, the restorer of streets to dwell in"

(Isaiah 58:12). Words like, "build," raise up foundations," "many generations," "repairer," and, "restorer." There are some "construction activities" taking place in this verse! There are foundations to be established for future generations.

When I noticed these words, I realized that probably this chapter was not only talking about fasting, but more like, "The benefits or the victories that can be received by those who will know and obey God." These same people shall become the generation that shall build old waste place and also raise a foundation of many generations. In other words, these are people who will be so much Kingdom minded that they will not just live for themselves but more for the Lord and for other people, both in the now and into the future; that they will definitely impact future generations. I now realized that probably verse twelve of Isaiah chapter fifty-eight was one of the most powerful verses in this whole passage. Of course I need to mention that for the original Israelite, they may have understood this passage to refer to the rebuilding of either the city of Jerusalem or the other cities that had to be rebuilt after the captivity.

As for the meeting in Pittsburgh, I realized why the Lord would have Rev. Shirley Brown ask me to speak from Isaiah fifty-eight. The Lord was affirming and encouraging this woman of God for her place and zeal in "Raising a foundation that will benefit many generations." He also gave me that message so that the person reading this book could benefit from the same. God is awesome!

I called my message that day, "Raising a foundation for many generations." That morning as I stood in Pittsburg I felt completely at ease as I shared on this message that I will now share with you.

If you have read this book from the beginning then you'll understand why I included the issue of raising foundations for many generations. Caleb the son of Jephunneh would have received this same kind of commendation. He was the man who raised a foundation of many generations. God Himself had promised him that He would cause him to inherit the land of promise. More than his personal inheritance was the fact that all his future generations would benefit from his faithfulness. The message that Caleb received from the Lord compares very well to what this chapter is about. He was being called to lay a foundation that would impact future generations.

Cry aloud!

The first message in Isaiah 58 is a call to God's people to raise their voices as trumpets and tell His people to repent. God says, "Tell my people their transgressions and the house of Jacob their sins" (Isaiah 58:1). It is clear all through the scriptures and not only in this one chapter that if God were to establish a solid foundation in His people; a foundation that will also be a blessing for the future generations; it has to begin with repentance. The scriptures command us to keep our hearts with all diligence, for out of it spring the issues of life (Proverbs 4:23). Each of us has to guard and be very careful as to what we allow into our hearts. What we allow into our hearts becomes a controlling factor on what our future would become.

Right now I am thinking of that day forty-six years ago when I stood in a Revival meeting in Mama Margaret's house in the village of Korio, Kenya. The change that took place in my life when I asked Christ to come into my heart and to forgive all my sins is what has made me who I am today. Actually even some of the schools I have attended, the places I have gone, the wife I married, and the way we raised our children, were all determined by that one change that took place when I repented of my sins and asked Jesus to come into my heart and take residence in me. The words of 2 Corinthians 5:17 became a reality in me. I became a new creation in Jesus Christ. That change determined the direction my life would take for the rest of my days.

Repentance is foundational

Repentance then is the beginning of a relationship with the Father. I think I cannot emphasize enough the message of repentance. It's hard to believe how very few preachers still preach on repentance. Actually, in many churches the preachers have changed the language in their preaching. The general feeling in many circles, especially in the Western world is that the preaching of sin and repentance will be offensive to the listeners. Guess what? Every true prophet in the scriptures, even the Apostles of our Lord and our Lord Himself offended a lot of people. None of these prophets and apostle would back up or change their message because someone was offended!

This reminds me of a story I heard from the Anglican Bishop David Gitari when I was a teenager in the mid-seventies. I attended a youth camp organized by the Kenya Students Christian Fellowship at the Alliance Boys School near Nairobi. At that time a prominent politician had just been assassinated. After the assassination, Bishop Gitari preached a message on radio about the sacredness of the human life and how nobody had the right to kill someone else, whatever their state or position in life was. This message seemed to irritate some top government leaders in our country. A few days after his message, he received a visit from some government special branch people. They warned him about his preaching. "The message you preached the other day on radio was very disturbing. You should not preach such a message in a time like this!" they snarled at him. The man of God then answered them quickly and firmly, "Indeed the message of the cross is disturbing especially to sinners like you!"

Another story of a similar kind took place in the nation of Israel during the prophetic ministry of Amos. The Lord sent him to go to the Northern kingdom of Israel and prophecy against the false altars that Jeroboam and set up. When Amos got to the North, he preached powerfully and prophesied against the false religious practices and against the ungodly leaderships that had been set up by King Jeroboam. His message incensed Amaziah, the senior priest at Bethel. He reported Amos to the King. "Amos has conspired against you in the midst of the house of Israel. The land is not able to bear all his words" (Amos 7:10).

Amos did not retreat or cower in fear just because the priest had reported him to the King. He answered the priest, "I was not a prophet, nor was I a son of a prophet, but I was a sheep breeder and a tender of sycamore fruit. Then the Lord took me as I followed the flock, and the Lord said to me, 'Go prophesy to my people Israel" (Amos 7:14).

What the prophet was telling this false preacher was, "The message I am preaching is not about me or from me. It has a divine origin. God, Himself sent and authorized me to do what I am doing and therefore I cannot retreat!"

This could be your message today. Are you facing some challenges and oppositions in your ministry? Do you feel like giving up because of the heat of opposition? Please stand firm and see the salvation of the Lord; He has not left you. He will see you through. C. John Miller explains that by being steadfast and standing for that which is right, the unbelievers will often be drawn to such a life even though they may not understand what the drawing power is. "They can sense the presence of God when Christians surrender their hearts to the Father–including their self-stained virtues, skills and knowledge" (*Repentance*, 87).

They Never gave Up

The prophets and apostles continued preaching even when at times their preaching attracted negative reactions from the hearers. Sometimes, as in the case of Amos, they put their lives at stake. They were bold and courageous as they faced great opposition. They continued preaching God's word to His people fearlessly.

Even the Apostles were warned about preaching in the Name of Jesus. Their message included repentance and a challenge for their hearers to recognize that Jesus is the Son of God and the Lord of glory. The Jewish leadership threatened them and commanded them not to preach in the Name of Jesus. They responded by telling the members of the Sanhedrin, "Whether it is right in the sight of God to listen to you more than to God, you judge. For we cannot but speak the things which we have seen and heard" (Acts 4:19-20).

These apostles did not compromise; opposition did not mean stopping or diluting their message. When opposition comes our way, the temptation is to quit or change the message. Not so for the prophets and our first century brothers and sisters. They stood firm in the worst of times and testified of God's saving grace.

These prophets and apostle understood that God's way and His word has no multiple choices. It is either you follow Him and obey His word or you don't. Actually, God has never tolerated lukewarmness. The church of Laodicea was to be spit out of God's mouth for their pride and arrogance, which had led to lukewarmness (Revelation 3:14-22).

A Holy God

As mentioned earlier God wants to have an intimate relationship with His people and the only way that relationship can be established is by acknowledging His holiness, recognize our sinfulness, and be willing to repent and forsake our sinfulness. That's why in Isaiah fifty-eight the first challenge for the servants of God is to cry aloud and warn God's people of their transgressions. Isaiah uses the title, "The Holy One of Israel" throughout his book. Hill observes, "This title not only shows Isaiah's emphasis on the holiness of God, but also reflects the books concern over the seriousness of Israel's offense against the God" (A survey, 325).

When you read the Bible, you'll find scores of verses that talk of God's holiness. Actually passages in the Old Testament call God, "The Holy One of Israel" (Hebrew: "***K'dosh Yisrael***"). (See 2 Kings 19:22, Psalms 71:22, Isaiah 1:4, 5:19, Jeremiah 50:29). Isaiah saw the Seraphim in heaven crying one to another, "Holy, Holy, Holy is the Lord of Hosts; the whole earth is full of His glory (Isaiah 6:3). The four living creatures in heaven also worship the Lord and say, "Holy, Holy, Holy, Lord God Almighty, Who was, and is and is to come" (Revelation 4:8).

He Knows our Frame

Our God is a holy God who also hates sin, but has never left the human race by themselves. He loves us and knows our frame; and remembers that we are dust (Psalm 103:14). He also knows that our own righteousness is like filthy rags before Him, and that there is none that is righteous, no not one (See Isaiah 64: 6, Romans 3:10). When we are left to ourselves we tend to stray like sheep without a shepherd.

This is why Jesus put on the human nature, so that He can fully identify and sympathize with our weaknesses. "Inasmuch then as the children have partaken of flesh and blood, He Himself likewise shared in the same, that through death He might destroy him who had the power of death, that is, the devil, and release those who through fear of death were all their lifetime subject to bondage. For indeed He does not give aid to angels, but He does give aid to the seed of Abraham. Therefore, in all things He had to be made like *His* brethren, that He might be a merciful and faithful High Priest in things *pertaining* to God, to make propitiation for the sins of the people. For in that He Himself has suffered, being tempted, He is able to aid those who are tempted (Hebrews 2:14-18).

Divine Invitation

When God says, "Cry aloud," it is because of His great love and concern for His people. In other words He is saying, "I love you so much that I am commanding my servants to do the best they can–to utilize every means possible for you to come to the knowledge of God." In Isaiah 1:8, God invites us to come and have a dialogue with Him. "Come now, and let us reason together," says the Lord, 'though your sins are like scarlet, they shall be as white as snow; though they are red like crimson, they shall be as wool."

In this passage God promises that whatever our sins are, and however deep in sin, He is able to cleanse us and make us completely whole. He will never leave us in our sins, as long as we are willing to respond to His divine invitation. His love and mercy are boundless. You are never too sinful to come to Him for forgiveness. 1 John 1:9 says, "If we confess our sins, He is faithful and just to forgive us our sins and to cleanse us from all unrighteousness." This is a great promise. God will cleanse every sin that is confessed to Him, as long as we come to Him with broken and contrite hearts. David says, "A broken and a contrite heart–these O God, you will not despise" (Psalm 51:17b).

According to J. I Packer, believers, "are called to a life of habitual repentance, as a discipline integral to healthy holy living" (Packer, 121). The more I serve the Lord, the more I am aware of my humanness, and the more I see the need for constant soul-searching and the need for repentance. I now know why St. Paul talked of dying daily (1 Corinthians 15:31).

When I worked as a Hospice chaplain, I came to know quite a few medical terms since I had to work constantly with Doctors and nurses. When a doctor gives a diagnosis of a particular cancer and says that it has metastasized, it's usually bad news. It means that the cancer has spread from the place where it first started to another place in the body. In other words that cancer is worse than it was before. This is the same situation in our spiritual lives. Unconfessed and un-repented sins will lead to spiritual metastasis. Such sin may eventually destroy you spiritually. If you have some sin that as it were has become part of your character, you'll need to repent, and at times you many need the support of a spiritual leaders who might help you seek God's help to overcome that particular sin.

A Broken and Contrite Heart

In the story of Caleb the son of Jephunneh God declared that this man had followed Him whole-heartedly (Numbers 14:24). To follow God whole-heartedly would also mean having a broken and contrite heart. This is the kind of heart that touches the Master when we call upon Him. He will never turn down a prayer offered in His will and from a broken and contrite heart.

I used to wonder why David enjoyed such great favor from the Father to the extent that even Jesus the Son of God is often referred to as "the Son of David. This is contrast with King Saul who was rejected of the Lord after failing to obey God just a couple of times. Saul's stubbornness and pride brought him down so fast! God cannot stand pride and arrogance. The bible says that God opposes the proud (James 4:6).

On the other hand someone would think that David received such favor and commendation from the Father because he was perfect and sinless. As we know from the scriptures, such was not the case. David was far from being perfect.

In actual fact David lusted, committed adultery, planned the murder of the woman's husband and then tried to cover the whole thing. However, we find that even though his relationship with the Father was marred by his sin, he knew how to return to the Lord in repentance. He knew the heart of the Father. He understood that our heavenly Father, not only knows our frame, but does relate or respond to us according to our human nature and experience. He says, "He has not dealt with us according to our sins, nor punished us according to our iniquities (Psalm 103:10). Mercy and grace are two great attributes which our heavenly Father releases to us when we have fallen short of His standards of holiness.

> Mercy and grace are two great attributes which our heavenly Father releases to us when we have fallen short of His standards of holiness.

David knew the attitude and the language that the Father would accept. It had to be an attitude of brokenness, humility and repentance. We find that after his sin with Bathsheba, he prayed, "Have mercy upon me, O God according to your lovingkindness. According to the multitude of your tender mercies blot out my transgressions. Wash me thoroughly from my iniquity and cleanse me from my sin. (Psalm 51:1-2).

David also understood that every sin that a person commits is an affront to the Holy God of Israel. He also knew that every sin is first and foremost against God. He said "Against you, you only have I sinned and done this evil in your sight. That you may be found just when you speak, and blameless when you judge (Psalm 51:4).

When any of us falls into any kind of sin, we need to hastily return to our loving heavenly Father for forgiveness. All He asks of us is broken and contrite hearts. Of course this does not mean that we make a mockery of His grace and forgiveness by living in sin and practicing all kind of ungodliness in order that we can always run to Him for forgiveness. Paul the apostle warns against such an attitude. "What shall we say then? Shall we continue in sin that grace may abound? Certainly not! How shall we who died to sin live any longer in it?" (Romans 6:1-2).

However, whenever you find yourself in a spiritual state that does not honor the Father, we do have a place of refuge to run and find full forgiveness and cleansing. "Seeing then that we have a great High Priest who has passed through the heavens, Jesus the Son of God, let us hold fast *our* confession. For we do not have a High Priest who cannot sympathize with our weaknesses, but was in all *points* tempted as *we are, yet* without sin" (Hebrews 4:14-15).

He invites you to Himself. "Come to Me, all *you* who labor and are heavy laden, and I will give you rest. Take My yoke upon you and learn from Me, for I am gentle and lowly in heart, and you will find rest for your souls" (Matthew 11:28-29).

Lesson from Chapter 9

NO ONE EVER gains a full and perfect knowledge of God and His will while here on earth. This is why faith is so important to a believer. There are scores of things in the Word that you may never know fully, but you just accept them by faith.

Each of us has to guard and be very careful as to what we allow into our hearts. What we allow into our hearts becomes a controlling factor of what our future will become.

The Old Testament prophets and the New Testament Apostle understood that God's way and His word has no multiple choices. It is either you follow Him and obey His word or you don't. God has never tolerated lukewarmness.

Our God is a holy God who also hates sin, but has never left the human race by themselves. He loves us and knows our frame; and remembers that we are dust (Psalm 103:14).

God will never leave us in our sins, as long as we are willing to respond to His divine invitation. His love and mercy are boundless. You are never too sinful to come to Him for forgiveness.

If you have some sin that as it were has become part of your character, you'll need to repent, and at times you many need the support of a spiritual leaders who might help you seek God's help to overcome that particular sin.

Mercy and grace are two great attributes which our heavenly Father releases to us when we have fallen short of His standards of holiness.

When any of us falls into any kind of sin, we need to hastily return to our loving heavenly Father for forgiveness. All He asks of us is broken and contrite hearts.

Armstrong Cheggeh

Chapter 10

Raising the Foundation for Many Generations (Part 2)

> *"Those from among you shall build the old waste places; you shall raise up the foundations of many generations; and you shall be called the repairer of the breach, the restorer of streets to dwell in"*
> *(Isaiah 58:12).*

AS MENTIONED IN the previous chapter, I read the words of Isaiah 58, verse twelve, as I was preparing to go and speak in that meeting in Pittsburgh, Pennsylvania. Something "jumped out" from the page. I read it several times, and realized that even though I had preached from this chapter many times, I had never noticed this verse. I then went on and did a thorough study of the whole passage as to get the greater idea or the teaching in this chapter.

God had rejected the prayers and fasting of the children of Israel. They asked the Lord why He would reject their prayers, and especially because it was accompanied by fasting. The Lord was kind enough to respond to them, and explain why He could not accept both their prayers and their fasting (See Isaiah 58:3-7). We will discuss God's answer about fasting to Israel, but I want to begin with Christ's teaching on fasting. There are some in the

Christian world who question whether fasting is a necessary practice in the New Testament, and especially for today.

The Right way to Fast

Our Lord Jesus addressed the subject of fasting a few times in His teachings. In His day the subject of fasting was not a new thing. The Jewish people practiced fasting, even as we can see in Isaiah fifty-eight. The teaching of fasting is not only to be found in the Old Testament, but also in the New Testament. It is mentioned approximately thirty-one times in twenty-six verses in the New Testament. The saints of both the Old and New Testaments practiced fasting.

Therefore, when Jesus taught on fasting, He was not introducing a new doctrine, but rather explaining the proper way to utilize the discipline of fasting especially for His followers. He said, "Moreover, when you fast, do not be like the hypocrites, with a sad countenance, for they disfigure their faces that they may appear to men to be fasting, assuredly, I say to you, they have their reward" (Matthew 5:16). We note in this passage that Jesus did not say, "If you fast," but rather, "When you fast." In other words, Jesus expected His followers to practice prayer and fasting.

Power of Prayer and Fasting

In another instance Jesus demonstrated to His disciples the power behind prayer and fasting. This happened after the great event of the mountain of transfiguration. Jesus and three of his disciples, Peter, James, and John came from the mountain only to find the other nine disciples very frustrated. They were surrounded by a group of people who must have been mocking and laughing at them because they had just failed to cast out a demon from a young man. This young man, according to his father had been oppressed of the devil since childhood. The Apostles of Jesus were most likely the best and greatest of the preachers of the day because they were taught by the Master Himself; yet they could not cast this particular demon!

In Mark 9: 28, they asked Jesus, "Why could we not cast it out? This question shows that they were surprised and probably confused as to why this particular demon did not obey them.

First, upon his return from the mountain, Jesus had rebuked his disciples for their unbelief, which leads me to emphasize a very important biblical principle. Without faith, whatever action, ritual, and ceremony we perform will not avail much. Even before Christ would teach His disciples of the value of prayer and fasting, He challenged them of the need to have faith if they would see results in their ministries. Faith is indeed the key to all the treasures in the Kingdom of God. The Bible says that without faith it is impossible to please God (Hebrews 11:6). There are so many things you can do without in God's Kingdom, but faith is indeed an imperative. It is impossible to serve the Lord without faith. Faith is a requirement in all of the services we render in the kingdom.

> Without faith, whatever action, ritual, and ceremony we perform will not avail much.

After the people had departed, the disciples asked the Lord the reason why they were unable to cast out the demon. Apparently they were so embarrassed that they waited until everybody had left before asking this question (Mark 9:28).

Jesus answered them; "This kind can come out by nothing but prayer and fasting (Mark 9:29). By this statement, Jesus demonstrated that just as in the Kingdom of God, the devil's kingdom too, has ranks and a hierarchy of demonic forces. Demons are in different levels and rank. In Ephesians 6:12 the bible says that we do not wrestle against flesh and blood, but against principalities, against powers, against the rulers of the darkness of this age, against spiritual hosts of wickedness in the heavenly places.

Power over Demonic Forces

There are some mighty demonic forces that have greater power and influence than the junior spirits. This is why Jesus would say, "this kind," meaning that these particular demons were stronger or of a higher rank than other junior demons. In Ephesians chapter six, Paul is talking about four levels in the enemy's hierarchy or ranks. He reminds the believers that their warfare is not a physical one, but a war against spiritual forces. "Paul clarifies here that the opposition is not one powerful supernatural being, but a whole range of evil forces of varying rank, authority, and capability" (Arnold, 447). Paul mentions, "Principalities", (Greek: "***Arche***"). This word means, "chief, in order, time, place or rank" (Strong, Greek, 92). These are preeminent demons or rulers. These are chief or high ranking demonic entities with their own territories (Romans 8:38, Ephesians 3:10, Colossians 1:16, 2:15, Titus 3:1**)**. These principalities are ruling demonic spirits possessing executive authority or governmental rule in the world. These principalities are usually given rule by the devil over a particular tribe, nation, people or race – these are more like the devil's ambassadors.

We see the operation of such a demonic principality in the book of Daniel. When the angel came to Daniel in response to his prayers, he explained that he would have brought the answer sooner were it not for the delay brought about by the opposition from a demonic principality called, "Prince of the kingdom of Persia." He also explained that he was only successful because a mightier angel by the name Michael came to his aid against this powerful demonic principality (Daniel 10:12-13). The teaching in this passage is in line with the words of Jesus of Mark 9:29, when He talked of "this kind." Definitely, there are demons that are more powerful than others, and who are harder to deal with than junior demons.

However, It is important though, to understand that, there is not one demon, however powerful that can overcome the power of intense prayers, especially when accompanied by fasting. This is especially true when the saints join up in what is called joint prayer and fasting as we shall see later. Jentezen reminds us that "Fasting is a tremendous weapon and a source of power in the life of a believer "(Jentezen, 49).

Leaving Behind a Righteous Legacy

The second group is the "Powers" (Greek: *"Exousia"*). The word Exousia, means, "derived or conferred authority, the warrant or right to do something, or delegated influences and control." (Luke 12:11, Ephesians 3:10, Colossians 1:16, 2:15). These are described as powers or authorities. These are superhuman, potentate with delegated influence, authority, or jurisdiction.

In keeping with the context of Ephesians 6:12, this group would include all high-ranking, evil supernatural powers and the power of sin and evil in operation in the world. These are the demonic powers that govern most institutions in this world. No wonder our brother John warns the believers about loving the world and the things in the world (1 John 2:15). "Do not love the world or the things in the world. If anyone loves the world, the love of the Father is not in him."

> However, it is important though, to understand that, there is not one demon, however powerful can overcome the power of intense prayers, especially when accompanied by fasting.

If you love the world and the things of the world you will find yourself being controlled by the demonic *Exousia*. Thank God, that by His power and love He has delivered us from the Exousia of darkness and conveyed us into the Kingdom of the Son of His love, in whom we have redemption through His blood, the forgiveness of sins (Colossians 1:13).

The third group, are the "Rulers of darkness." (Greek: "**Kosmokratoras**"). These are cosmic powers or worldly powers. **Kosmos** does not mean only the people of the world but the system of the world. Therefore, these world rulers are associated with magic and demonic gods such as were found in the idolatry in Ephesus, and even in our present world. These are spiritual forces that also control evil in the heavenly realm.

Finally, he mentions the "Spiritual host of wickedness in high places." (Greek: **Pneumatikos**). In describing these forth group of demonic spirits he uses the Greek word, *"poneria,"* which means depravity and particularly in the sense of malice and mischief, plots, sins, and iniquity (Strong, *Exhaustive*, 59). These are spirit forces of perniciousness in the heavenly places. They are spiritual hosts of wickedness or spiritual forces of evil.

For now I will not go into details about the operations of these spiritual forces and our victory over them. In the near future I plan to do more research and write on the subject of spiritual warfare, but right now I want to concentrate on the subject of prayer and fasting. My point here is to point out that Jesus taught that prayer and fasting does aid in breaking the power of even the worst and the most powerful of these spiritual forces (Mark 9:29). It is also to point out that our Lord expects his followers to practice prayer and fasting. He said, "When you fast" (Matthew 6:16-18). He did not say, "If you fast." He expects the believers to practice prayer and fasting. He expects you to practice prayer and fasting. Personally I cannot imagine a believer's life without prayer and fasting.

> You would have to look long and hard in the history of the church to see any great man or woman of God who did not practice prayer and fasting.

I am reminded of that anointed preacher John Wesley, who was also the founder of the Methodist Church. He loved the Lord with all his heart and practiced prayer and fasting regularly. God used him mightily to bring thousands of people into the Kingdom of God. He believed that fasting brought blessing to those who practiced it (Wesley, *The Sum*, 124, 133). He valued prayer and fasting to the extent that he could not imagine a believer, and especially a preacher continuing with their service without prayer and fasting. He would, therefore not ordain any preacher who did not practice prayer and fasting. That's how much he valued the practice of prayer and fasting. You would have to look long and hard in the history of the church to see any great man or woman of God who did not practice prayer and fasting.

Not for Strive and Debate

In Isaiah 58:4, the Lord castigates the nation of Israel for strive and debate while they fasted. Apparently, they were more interested in comparing, contrasting, and even competing to see who would fast longer or better. Probably they even compared notes as to who received the greater outcome of blessing from his time of fasting.

Their fasting was no longer about serving God and having a good relationship with Him, but rather serving self. Instead of walking in humility as they sought the Lord in prayer and fasting, they were being proud and arrogant as they compared their spirituality with each other.

Fasting for Show!

So we find that the next thing that the Lord rebuked them for, was fasting in such a way as to impress other people. God asked, "Is it a fast that I have chosen, a day for a man to afflict his soul? Is it to bow down his head like a bulrush, and to spread sackcloth and ashes? Would you call this a fast and an acceptable day of the Lord? (Isaiah 58:5).

These people behaved in such a way as to show other people how spiritual they were. God, His Kingdom and the walk of faith were no longer their priority. Getting a big name and religious recognition were of paramount importance to them. They were looking for the praise of men. That is why they would walk with their heads bowed down as a bulrush, as to say, "See how holy and serious I am in my walk with God. I have been fasting for such a long time and that is why I am this weak. I cannot stand straight, and have to hung my head as a bulrush!" The Lord wanted people who would fast with the right attitude. "God wants humility in the bringing of one's request to Him, in knowing His will, cherishing it, and imbibing it as one losing himself in the wonder of it. He wants us to seek His will in complete surrender to His love and purposes" (Shackelford, 582).

When Jesus taught on fasting, He told his disciples that they should never fast for show. It should never be done for the praise of men. He said, "Moreover, when you fast do not be like the hypocrites, with a sad countenance, for they disfigure their faces that they may appear to men to be fasting (Matthew 6:16).

Basically, the practice of fasting is between the individual believer and the heavenly Father. Jesus promised that if only we can fast with sincerity of heart and as unto the Lord, then "Your Father who sees in secret will reward you openly (Matthew 6:18). Serious prayer and fasting that is done from a sincere heart will never go unnoticed by our heavenly Father.

I should mention here that fasting in secret does not necessarily mean that nobody will know you are fasting. If you are living with other people in the same house, and especially if you are husband and wife, one of you will definitely know when the other one is fasting. Actually, as for spouses the bible makes it clear that you will have to inform each other when one of you is fasting, especially if the fasting includes abstaining from sexual relations with your spouse (1 Corinthians 7:5).

Therefore, the idea is not necessarily that you keep it a secret, but that it should not be for the praise of men. All fasting should be as unto the Lord. There are very few times that you can fast without other people knowing that you are fasting, unless you live by yourself or you opt to go for a retreat away from people.

I was deeply impressed by our brothers and sisters in South Korea. These believers have built places they call, "Prayer Mountains." The believers visit these places often and spend days in prayer and fasting. In Kenya, we do have a few special places that have been established just for prayer and fasting. Such places are great for prayer retreats. When you visit such places for three days or for a week, you return home or to your ministry renewed and spiritually invigorated. Such prayer retreats have been a great blessing to my life. I cannot exchange my experiences at those "prayer mountains" with any other spiritual experience.

Joint Prayer and Fasting

There are also times when a group of people decide to pray and fast together. Of course if you are praying and fasting as a group, everybody in the group will know that the others are fasting. This idea of people praying corporately was practiced in both the Old and New Testament. In our day and time, a particular church or fellowship may have an issue that they consider very crucial to the running of the ministry. They may also be facing some national disasters or great political transitions. During such times, the church may decide to pray and fast together, either as a congregation or sometimes call for a national day of prayer and fasting. Such great joint prayer and fasting produces great spiritual breakthroughs.

Having been born and raised in Kenya, I personally believe that if it were not for the intense prayer and fasting that many of the believers in our country prayed before general elections, our countries would have sunk into great chaos and turmoil. Somehow the strongholds of tribalism and nepotism have had great sway for many of the African nations. We still have a long way to go before our people see themselves as a nation and not as little tribes with a lot of ethnocentric mind-sets and pride. However, we cannot give up to the spirit of apathy and pessimism. God is able to change not only individuals, but also whole nations. He is, however, looking for a man and woman to stand in the gap for these nations through prayer and fasting.

Most modern-day preachers do not preach on prayer and fasting. The enemy of our souls seems to have blinded them as to the importance and power that comes from prayer and fasting. If the whole body of Christ were to rise to the challenge of prayer and fasting, there is no telling the kinds of spiritual breakthroughs we would experience.

All Great Warriors Fast

It is important to note that the greatest of God's warriors were people who practiced prayer and fasting. Moses (Exodus 24:18, 34:28, Deuteronomy 9:9, 18, 25-29, 10:10), Elijah (1 Kings 19:8), David, the man after God's own heart fasted (Psalm 35:13, 11 Samuel 12:15-23). Daniel, the prophet with an excellent spirit prayed and fasted often (Daniel 9:3). Nehemiah the leader, who rebuilt the city of Jerusalem, fasted often (Nehemiah 1:4, 9:1-3). Paul, the great Apostle fasted often and considered fasting as a very crucial part of his ministry (11 Corinthians 6:4-10, 11:23-28). Our Lord, Himself spent time in prayer and fasting (Matthew 4:2, Mark 1:13, Luke 4:2).

The Jewish people prayed and fasted when their enemy Herman planned to annihilate them. God intervened and brought great victory for the Jewish people (Esther 4:15-17). The early church also practiced prayer and fasting. Sometimes they prayed and fasted individually (Acts 9:9, 10:1-4, 30-31), and other times they prayed and fasted as a group (Acts 13:1-3, 14:23).

Fasting and Repentance

In Joel 2:12, the Lord tells the nation of Israel, "Now, therefore', says the Lord, 'Turn to me with all your heart, with fasting, with weeping and with mourning. So rend your heart, and not your garments; return to the Lord your God, for He is gracious and merciful, slow to anger, and of great kindness; and He relents from doing harm"

In the story of Jonah, God turned his wrath from the city of Nineveh when the whole population of the city turned to God and repented as they prayed and fasted (Jonah 3:8).

I believe that even as of today, the nation that would turn to God in repentance with prayer and fasting would experience the Hand of God in a big way. If the church would learn and appreciate the power of prayer and fasting, it would experience great breakthroughs in every aspect of its life.

The early church understood this power so much so, that as they sent out the first missionaries from the church of Antioch, they prayed and fasted before they commissioned them (Acts 13:1-3). Even as they ordained church leaders they first of all spent time in prayer and fasting (Acts 14:23). The early church spent time in prayer and fasting when facing a crisis or in times of transitions. Can we do any less?

The Scriptures say that we are built on the foundation of the Apostles and prophets, with our Lord Jesus as the chief cornerstone (Ephesians 2:20). If then we are built on the foundation of the Apostles and prophets, wouldn't it make sense that we would want to walk the path that they walked, and especially when we realize that it was our Lord's desire that His followers to be men and women of prayer and fasting (Matthew 6:16-18, 9:14-15).

God showed the people in Isaiah's day the value of not only prayer and fasting, but also the need to fast with the right attitude. We, too, need to be reminded that prayer and fasting without sincerity of heart will not avail much. Just like in the words of David, it is a contrite and broken heart that gets a positive response from our heavenly Father (Psalm 51:17).

Absolute or Complete Fasting

There are different kinds of fasts. One of these is called, "Absolute" or "complete fast." Some people like to call it "dry fasting." This is where the individual believer does not eat or drink anything.

This is the kind of fast that queen Esther requested from the Jewish people for a period of three days (Esther 4:16). She said, "Go gather all the Jews who are present in Shushan, and fast for me; neither eat or drink for three days, night or day. My maids and I will fast likewise. And so I will go to the king, which is against the law; and if I perish, I perish!"

Normally this kind of fast should not be longer than three to four days. I have heard of at least three brothers who have died as a result of doing a long absolute fast. It is very important that we do not fast more than three to four days when doing an absolute fast. You are not fasting to kill yourself! Fasting should never be a suicide attempt!

Regular or Normal Fasting

Regular fasting is when an individual or a group of believers abstain from solid foods but drink fluids as they fast. This kind of fast can last from one day to forty days. This is the most common fast among believers, and which the author would recommend for believers to practice often.

Actually when I pastored the church in Nairobi I used to encourage our members to consider fasting at least a few days per month. You can choose to be fasting for one to three days or so per month.

Partial Fasting – The Daniel's Fast

Partial fasting is when someone abstains from certain foods, but continues to eat other foods. Daniel the prophet practiced this kind of fast, and that's why many people call partial fasting, "the Daniel's fast." He says, "In those days, I, Daniel was mourning three full weeks, I ate no pleasant food, no meat or wines came into my mouth, nor did I anoint myself at all, till three whole weeks were fulfilled" (Daniel 10:2-3).

I have known bible school student who will agree as a group to fast certain foods so that the funds, which would have been used to prepare the food, would be sent to a particular project in the mission field.

There are times when people fast a particular food in order to be reminded of God's goodness and provision or in order to identify with their brothers and sisters in poorer nations. For example in the western world where food is plenty, the believers will fast certain foods like meat to remind themselves of their brothers and sister in foreign lands who are going through droughts and famines. They will then be reminded when they miss these foods to pray for their brothers across the world, and sometimes to contribute funds in support of their brothers and sisters in these foreign lands.

Purposes of Fasting

Humility and Repentance: One of the reasons we fast is to humble ourselves before our heavenly Father (Ezra 8:21, Joel 2:12, Psalm 35:13).

Sharing: We also fast so that we can share our resources with the poor, the naked, and the oppressed (Isaiah 58:6-7).

Commissioning and getting ready for service: The church prayed and fasted before commissioning Paul and Barnabas (Acts 13:1-3).

Transition or crisis: There are times we fast when going through some major transition in life or a crisis (Nehemiah 1:4, Judges 20:26).

Intercession: There are times that individuals, a small group or a local church will fast to intercede for their nation. This is more like what Esther did or what the people of Nineveh did (Esther 4:16, Jonah 3:5-9).

Deliverance: Jesus said that some demons would not come out unless the believers pray and fasts (Mark 9:29). When the church engages in prayer and fasting, it gains great spiritual authority and will see greater fruit in that people will receive deliverance from the bondage of the enemy.

A word of Advice to Church Leaders

Fasting is such a challenging discipline. It really helps to have some plan or schedule if you are to fast regularly. Usually if you as a leader say that you will fast without setting a particular time, you will find that something seems to always come that causes you not to fast. The best thing to do then is to place the dates you want to fast in your diary or calendar.

For example, when I was the lead pastor at one local church in Nairobi, I not only prayed and fasted alone, but on three occasions per year I involved the congregations in a joint prayer and fasting. We practiced it for several years until the members came to know that these were the seasons of our prayer and fasting and looked forward to those seasons. Normally we did a joint prayer and fasting for ten days at beginning of January. We would fast from the 2nd to the 11th of January every year. Some people would fast the whole ten days, while others did one day, two days, etc. No one was forced to take part, but those who did, had to sign their names on a list so that we would be sure that every day was covered. That is why I said previously that it is not necessary that other people would not know that you are fasting. The question is on the attitude each of us has while we are fasting.

We then did a 21-day fast in the month of April or May, and finally around November we closed the year with a 40-day fast. Again for both the 21-day and the 40-day fast only a few people did all the days. Most of the people did one to three days.

Because of placing it in the calendar it was very easy for most of us to take part in this joint-prayer and fasting. Once you have placed it in your calendar or diary, it becomes much easier to follow through with your season of fasting. Personally, I have realized that once I have placed my days of fasting in my diary, I end up carrying it through, while on the other hand if I say, "I will fast sometime," I find myself not fasting.

Even if you're going to fast alone, it still is important that you note the dates you want to fast in a notebook or diary. These days we even have electronic gadgets that can help you remember whatever event you want them to remind you.

Can you imagine the power the church would have if most of us would commit ourselves to seasons of prayer and fasting throughout the year? I believe that the great power and anointing experienced by our brothers and sisters in the first century of the church was hinged on their lives of prayers and fasting.

Faith that Works

Prophet Isaiah tells the Israelites that while they fasted, they should also seek to feed the hungry, support the poor people, and also dress the naked.

Isaiah's message is similar to that of Apostle James in the New Testament. James tells the early church that faith without works is dead (James 2:17). Isaiah says that fasting without works is a vain thing (Isaiah 58:3-7). The call here is to live a practical Christian life. We should live a life that is observable to the outside world. The world cannot see the faith in our hearts, but they definitely can see our lifestyles and how we relate to those around us.

It really does not matter how often or for how long we fast if we do not touch the lives of the people around us. Christianity is not a passive, empty religion. It is a living faith that ministers grace and life to those we encounters with daily. If our faith does not move us to be involved positively in the lives of other people, then we definitely need to examine our faith and our priorities.

> Christianity is not a passive, empty religion. It is a living faith that minsters grace and life to those who we encounter with daily.

The scriptures are clear about this subject. Paul told the believers at Corinth, "And He died for all, that those who live should live no longer for themselves, but for Him who died for them and rose again" (2 Corinthians 5:15). After you have come to Christ, you can no longer live just for yourself. First you live for Christ and His eternal glory, and then you allow Him to use you to touch those around you by His love.

When I first came to Christ forty-six years ago, there was a song that used to move me to tears when I thought of my responsibility to the people around me. One of the verses of this song says:

> *I gave my life for thee, My precious blood I shed,*
> *That thou might ransomed be, and raised up from the dead*
> *I gave my life for thee, what hast thou given for me?*
> *I gave my life for thee, what hast thou given for me?*
>
> *(Francis R Havergal, 1858 - Public domain)*

Another Faith

It is very possible to have "another faith." Just because someone claims to have faith does not mean that they have the true biblical faith. Biblical faith has to have the Word of God as it its foundation. We need to know that the source of true faith is God's word. The Bible says, "So then faith comes by hearing, and hearing by the Word of God (Romans 10:17). The more you read the scripture and listen to God's word, the more you are established in the faith.

I have heard of people who claim that nobody preached to them, and that they just prayed and got saved. While it is true that they prayed alone and asked Christ to come into their hearts, it is most probable that before that particular day, they had listened to a preacher either on Radio, Television or just in a revival meeting or Evangelistic crusade. What, therefore, happened, is that the Holy Spirit used the words they had heard to bring conviction into their lives, and thus they repented and received Christ as Savior of their lives. Saving faith comes to us only through the Word of God.

> After you have come to Christ, you will then understand that biblical faith will not allow you to live a life without positive actions and lifestyles that will show to the world that God's spirit is resident in your life.

After you have come to Christ, you will then understand that biblical faith will not allow you to live a life without positive actions and lifestyles that will show to the world that God's spirit is resident in your life. Jesus called this aspect of touching those around us," the Light and salt." "You are the salt of the earth; but if the salt loses its flavor, how shall it be seasoned? It is good for nothing but to be thrown out and trampled under food by men. You are the light of the world. A city on the hill cannot be hidden. Nor do they light a lamp and put it under a basket, but on a lamp stand, and it gives light to all who are in the house.' Let your light so shine before men, that they may see your good works and glorify your Father in heaven" (Matthew 5:13-16).

Do not tell me you are a believer unless your words and action also attest to the same. Even our Lord Jesus told those who questioned his authenticity, "The works that I do in my Father's Name, they bear witness of me," and then He added, "...though you do not believe me, believe the works, that you may know and believe that the Father is in me and I in Him (John 10:25, 38). In this passage, all that the Lord is saying is, "Since you do not seem to want to believe in what I say; believe then because of how I live. Believe because you have seen the fruit of my life." Jesus did not only talk the talk, he walked the walk. He demonstrated to those around Him how a life in the spirit is supposed to be lived.

Drawn by God

This partnership between the believer and our heavenly Father begins at the time we come to Him and continues on until our pilgrimage here on earth is ended. No one can come to Christ unless the Father draws him or her to Christ. Jesus says, "And I tell you that at no one can come to me unless it has been granted to him by My Father "(John 6:65). Also in John 15:16 He says, "You did not choose me, but I chose you and appointed you that you should go and bear fruit, and that you fruit should remain, that whatever you ask the Father in my Name He may give you."

You came to Christ not because you had such great spiritual sensitivity or such clear spiritual vision. You came to Christ because God by His grace and mercy drew you to Himself by the Holy Spirit. This, of course takes care of any pride and arrogance on our part! We all come to realize that all that we are, and ever hope to be, is all by God's grace and mercy.

One of the verses of the hymn, Rock of ages says:

> "Nothing in my hands I bring,
> Simply to the cross I cling;
> Naked, come to Thee for dress;
> Helpless, look to Thee for grace;
> Foul, I to the fountain fly;
> Wash me Savior, or I die.
>
> *(Augustus Montague Toplady, 1763 – Public domain)*

We need to respond with great humility, and a sense of responsibility when we realize that we owe everything we are and everything we have to God's grace and mercy.

Physical and Social Needs

If the Lord will entrust us with laying down a foundation that will bless future generations, as He did with Caleb the son of Jephunneh, we will need to be sensitive to what the Spirit is saying to the church concerning the needs of the people around us. God told the Israelites that the fasting that would impress him would be one where His people would be concerned and take responsibility of the needs of their fellow Israelites while they fasted.

> "Is it not to share your bread with the hungry,
> And that you bring to your house the poor who are cast out;
> When you see the naked, that you cover him,
> And not hide yourself from your own flesh?" (Isaiah 58:7).

As we minister physical needs to the people around us, they will most likely open up to our message of salvation. Actually, that's why the church is losing whole communities in the African continent to other faiths. When Muslims or any other religion, for that matter, builds a school or begins some feeding programs for some of the villages, you will find that the local people respond to their message positively. Their response is, "If you cared this much to feed me or to give me an education, you might as well have a message worth being listened to."

Many Evangelical and Charismatic groups have missed out on this dimension of ministry. I remember working with a certain denomination for quite some time. This particular denomination was quite Evangelical and did a lot of outreach ministries across the African continent. However, they did not have even one hospital, high school, or vocational school or college. They only had a number of bible schools. That is how much one-sided most African Evangelical and Charismatic ministries have become. These ministries are great in preaching the Word, but are very weak in meeting the physical and social needs to their communities.

Many in the Evangelical camp opposed the social gospel, which for a long time ignored the preaching of God's Word; and they were right, because we cannot replace the gospel of Christ with the social gospel. However, the Evangelicals on the other hand, have let the pendulum swing to the extreme side. They should have stopped in the middle ground, whereby they would preach the unadulterated Word of God and at the same time feed the hungry, visit the prisoners and the sick in Hospitals. They ought to be concerned about bringing clean water to those who do not have good water and also deal with the issues of illiteracy and health. The Evangelical and Charismatic churches have, therefore, ignored a very important aspect of the very faith they claim to defend–the issue of supporting the poor and the needy. Hansen explains that this is the message that the Lord was giving to the Israelites during the time of Isaiah. "The inseparability of worship from the life of justice and compassion thus is reaffirmed and held up as the only reliable foundation for a people trying to rebuild a nation after a period of calamity" (*Interpretation*, 206)

Both of these two aspects of ministry need to be highlighted, if the church of the twenty-first century is to prosper and flourish. You cannot preach to poor, hungry, naked people and expect them to respond well, unless you also address their physical and social needs.

A church that is weak in physical and social dimensions of the ministry will not stand the tides that are coming against the church today. On the other hand a ministry that will preach the unadulterated gospel with the power of the Holy Spirit and at the same time feed the hungry, dress the naked and visit the sick in hospitals and those in prison, will experience great growth and blessing. Remember the parable of the wedding feast (Matthew 22:1-14). The King is calling you and I to go to the highways and byways of life and compel the lost to come to the marriage feast. We cannot wait in the four walls of our churches and expect them to come. We can reach out to them through these outreach ministries which should include both the preaching of the gospel and meeting the physical and social needs of the people. Are you willing to obey His voice?

Ministry to the Whole Person

The church should, therefore, seek to minister to the whole person. An individual is not only a spirit, but has a soul, and a body. Each of these three dimensions of the human person ought to be ministered to.

As stated earlier, one of the greatest failures of many of the Evangelical, charismatic, or Pentecostal churches has been a complete disregard and disinterest in any of the physical and social needs of their communities and countries. Yet these same fellowships are great in the area of praise and worship and the preaching of God's word.

Of course no serious Christian would downplay the importance of preaching and praise and worship. These are important aspects of church life. However, a true church does not have only the dimension of praise and worship. It should have the dimension of caring for the needs of poor as well. Our brother

James called this kind of church, "the pure and undefiled religion" (James 1:27).

Our faith should have the dimension of caring for those suffering from AIDS, or caring for the children of the people who have died of AIDS. Such a church should have an outreach ministry to the prisons, to the hospitals, and also reach out to the refugees and those living in the poorer areas of the country.

We cannot just seat in our beautiful and comfortable churches singing, "O how I love Jesus!" If we so loved Jesus, why does it become so hard to honor Him and obey His voice, while He calls us to reach out to the needy people in our communities?

The challenge to care for the needy people is part of the message of Isaiah 58. God tells the Israelites, that if their fasting was to impress Him, they had to feed the hungry, cloth the naked, and stop oppressing their workers (Isaiah 58:6-7).

Can you imagine how fantastic and what an impact the church would have if every congregation and every believer would seek to touch others with the love of Jesus and be concerned of not only the salvation of their souls—even though this is of paramount importance, but also be concerned about their physical and social needs.

Plea for Widows

A few years ago the Lord spoke to me regarding the plight of the widows, especially in our African setting. Several young Kenyan preachers died within a period of five years. A few of these preachers who died were people I had known for many years. Some of them were personal friends.

I realized that when these young preachers died their wives and children suffered greatly because most churches in Africa and generally in most third world countries have no retirement plans or life insurance for the preachers. Even for those churches or denominations that have recently established a program to assist the families of the preachers, especially when the preacher is promoted to glory, have very little help for the pastors' families.

This reminds us the story we discussed in Chapter five of God's servant who died and his children were about to be sold into slavery (2 Kings 4:2-3). It was only after his widow pleaded with Elisha the man of God that these precious children escaped slavery.

Today, most of these preachers' children may not necessarily to be sold into slavery after their father dies, but in a way they are! They end up being "kicked" out of school for lack of school fees. Others go hungry or even lose their homes and have either to be raised by relatives or be totally dependent upon other people. Most of them are literally reduced to beggars.

The church leaders of Africa and most of the third world countries should open their spiritual ears to hear what the Spirit is saying to the churches. We cannot keep quiet when these precious sons and daughters and the widow of preachers are suffering.

You will notice that here I am pleading more for the women and children because generally in the third world countries men usually remarry soon after their wives pass away, and will normally keep the family property. However, for the women the situation is different. For example in my own tribe, when a woman gets married, the husband's family pays a dowry to the in-laws. This assures the husband's family that this woman will belong to their clan throughout her life. It does not matter whether the husband lives or dies; the woman belongs to the husband's family!

Of course things are changing fast. Recently a family member sought my advice about this issue. She wanted to marry her new fiancé several years after the husband had died. The husband's family would not hear of it! I consulted with other family members and we agreed that it was OK for her to marry her new fiancé. Of course this incensed most members of the in-laws, but she went ahead and got married. They now have a beautiful family.

Such is a very rare thing in the part of Africa I come from. Usually the woman remains single even if the husband dies when they are in their thirties or forties as was the case with the lady I mentioned above. Sometimes the men also will avoid these women because the community will always recognize them as belonging to their late husband's family.

Even with this claim of ownership on the part of the husband's family, very few of them take up the husband's responsibility. The woman usually takes up both her husband's role and her own role. This is usually very difficult especially if the husband was the breadwinner; which often is the case. For preachers' wives it is even worse because the husband is the preacher and so the wife most often will depend upon the husband's support while he lives. When a preacher dies, his family in most cases is left in a very difficult situation.

What can we do?

Praying for these widows and their children is important, but is not enough. Personally, what I have done in a couple of situations in Africa when a close ministry friend has died is to quickly call for a funds drive to support the family. Normally we announce the funds drive while the funeral is being planned and also on the day of the funeral. The reason we do this is because normally people promise all kinds of support for the family and yet they never even come to visit the family after the funeral.

The reality is that even those of us who are preachers have been found to be liars by promising to visit the bereaved families, and in most cases we do not. How many times have you heard people promising all kinds of support to the bereaved family during funerals? Normally they will say something like, "Please know that those of us who are your husband's friends will not forget or forsake you. We will be visiting your from time to time and please when you have any problems do not hesitate to contact any of us. We will be ready and willing to help." Normally very few people ever concern themselves with that family after the funeral, and even when they do, they do not support them in lasting, tangible ways. Most friends do not even return to that home ever!

I remember when a very popular preacher in Kenya died and everybody talked of how much they had loved him and how much they cared about his family. A short time later the wife was so frustrated because she could not afford to send her children to college and the very people who had talked of loving the husband and also being concerned of the family were nowhere to be seen!

The Sooner the Better

I, therefore, decided that the best solution was to do the best we can while we are still mourning and when the memory of the brother is still in our minds. You need to involve the family and friends when the pain and a sense of loss are still very real to all. Such a funds drive should be conducted not more than three months after the death of the servant of God, or for that matter any other person whether a preacher or not, whose family has been left in poverty.

I am not suggesting that this kind of support should be given only to the families of preachers, but more for any needy widows and orphans when the bread winner has passed away or when he has left a situation that will hinder his children from going on with school or if they will lose their house or land, as a result of the death. Do not promise to do anything if you are not willing to do it immediately or soon after the funeral. You have to hit the nail when it is hot. I know this part may not make a lot of sense to our brothers and sisters in the Western world, but in the third world countries, life insurance is out of question to the majority of the people. The fellowship of the saints becomes the life insurance to the members of the church.

My experience has shown me–and we have done this four times: when the funds drive is done within three months and is well orchestrated and of course led by someone that the community respects, people give generously and the family is well supported.

I know that there are some preachers reading this and

wondering why I should address this issue and not just pray that they may live and not die! Of course I wish that all preachers would live to be in their 80s and 90s. I pray that the Lord will give you a long life. However, the reality of life will show that some people will die in their 40s, 50s and even 60s. The preachers I mentioned earlier died before age 50 and yet every one of them was a wonderful preacher of the gospel. If and when that happens we should have a plan on how to support their widows and their children.

Retirement Funds

Another important step on the part of the Churches, and even for other organizations and businesses is for each to have a retirement program for their workers. Each of them should establish a solid, well-organized retirement program, which would benefit a pastor or Evangelist, or any other person working for them when they are older or support their families in case they die while in service. I know that I am emphasizing this point more for the African ministries and other third-world ministries than the Western ministries. Our Western brothers seem to be much more advanced in planning for their ministers than our African, Asian, and South American ministries.

Churches are good at raising funds and taking offerings. Of course we need funds for whatever work we need to accomplish here on earth for Kingdom purposes. The Bible says that money answers everything (Ecclesiastes 10:19). Of course money answers questions not only out in the world, but also in the church ministries. Even Jesus had a treasurer, although in this case he was a bad guy! We definitely need money for building churches, sending out missionaries, translating the Bible and numerous projects for the benefit of the churches we serve and the communities we live in.

Every church congregation or denomination should also acknowledge that the retirement fund of the pastors is also a very crucial and much needed aspect of the ministry. In our fellowship of churches we decided that on any given Sunday service, five per cent of the offering goes to the ministers' retirement fund. This will assure especially our young preachers that by the time they reach the age of fifty-five, which is the time this fund matures, they will have sufficient funds to take care of their families or to invest in some program that will be of help to them financially. This fund also can support the family if the pastor is called into the presence of the Lord, when he is young.

As mentioned above this fund matures when the Pastors are fifty-five years old, but does not mean that they retire then from preaching the gospel. Actually, our church has no real retirement age. We do not find a retirement age in the scriptures. What happens is that the pastors receive their benefits when they attain this age, but continue serving the Lord, and the local churches continue saving more funds for them as they continue serving. When the senior leaders of our church attain age seventy, then they retire from the administrative roles but not from the ministry. For example, any of the Presbyters and Bishops will serve until they are seventy; after this age, they are relieved of their administrative positions but they remain preachers in a local church, if they choose to. Some may choose not to have a church, but be available for other simpler ministries that they can do from time to time.

We still do not know the long-term implications of this retirement program since our fellowship of churches is pretty young, but we will keep improving it as time goes. We believe that this program will bring great blessings and stability to the families of the preachers both when they are older or even when any of them is promoted to glory. Any of the church leaders reading this and many have questions or may want further discussion on this subject may attend our annual leadership conferences or just invite the author to come and address this subject in your church or denominational conference (See contact information at the back pages of this book).

Please note that what we have done as a fellowship of churches can be done by other organizations and businesses. The idea here is that your workers need to be taken care of when they get older, or if they happen to die while still working for you.

If then as I said earlier, we are to become that generation that the Lord will entrust to establish a foundation for many generations (Isaiah 58:12), we need to consider how best to bless and minister to those who labor among us. This will definitely help them not to worry about their everyday needs, concentrate more on their ministries and thus be much more effective in what they do. In so doing, you will have established a good and solid foundation for future generations. Like Caleb these ministers will leave behind a strong legacy that will also be a blessing to their descendants.

The scriptures admonish us to give double honor to those Christian leaders who do their ministries well, especially when they labor in preaching the Word (1 Timothy 5:17). Paul also advises the believers at Galatia to share all good things with those who teach them the things of God (Galatians 6:6). He also reminded the Corinthians that God had commanded that those who preach the gospel should be supported by the ministries they serve (See 1 Corinthians 9:14).

> One of the ways that the believers can demonstrate their love for the Lord and the honor they have for His work is by supporting His servant regularly, and also by investing in a program that will help him or her when they get older.

One of the ways that the believers can demonstrate their love for the Lord and the honor they have for His work is by supporting His servant regularly, and also by investing in a program that will help him or her when they get older. This, the believers can do by being faithful in tithes and offerings, and also by establishing a retirement program either in their local church or on denominational level. That way the preacher will not suffer at old age and their families will not suffer unnecessarily if the Lord were to call His servant home.

Armstrong Cheggeh

Lessons from Chapter 10

WITHOUT FAITH, WHATEVER actions or rituals and ceremonies we perform will not avail much.

There is not one demon, however powerful that can overcome the power of intense prayers, especially when accompanied by fasting.

You would have to look hard in the history of the church to see any great man or woman of God who did not practice prayer and fasting.

The nation that would turn to God in repentance with prayer and fasting would experience the Hand of God.

Prayer and fasting without sincerity of heart will not avail much. Just like in the words of David, it is a contrite and broken heart that gets a positive response from our heavenly Father (Psalm 51:17).

It is very important that we do not fast more than three to four days when doing an absolute fast.

There are times when people fast a particular food in order to be reminded of God's goodness and provision or in order to identify with their brothers and sisters in poorer nations.

The great power and anointing experienced by our brothers and sisters in the New Testament times was hinged on their lives of prayers and fasting.

We should live a life that is observable to the outside world. The world cannot see the faith in our hearts, but they definitely can see our lifestyles and how we relate to those around us.

It really does not matter how often or for how long we fast if we do not touch the lives of the people around us. Christianity is not a passive, empty religion. It is a living faith that ministers grace and life to those we encounter with daily.

You came to Christ because God by His grace and mercy

drew you to Himself by the Holy Spirit. We all have to realize that all that we are and ever hope to be is because of God's grace and mercy.

The church should seek to minister to the whole person. An individual is not only a spirit, but has a soul, and a body.

A church that is weak in physical and social dimensions of the ministry will not stand the tides that are coming against the church today.

Every church congregation or denomination should also acknowledge that the retirement fund of the pastors is also a very crucial and much needed aspect of the ministry.

One of the ways that the believers can demonstrate their love for the Lord and the honor they have for His work is by supporting His servant regularly, and also by investing in a program that will help him or her when they get older.

Chapter 11

Repentance brings Healing

WHEN SOLOMON PRAYED that great prayer at the dedication of the temple in Jerusalem, he asked that God would respond to the cry of His people when confronted by enemies, during a drought and famine or whatever challenge the nation would encounter. God responded immediately with these words, "If my people who are called by My Name will humble themselves and pray and seek my face and turn from their wicked ways, then I will hear from heaven, and will forgive their sin and heal their land" (2 Chronicles 7:14).

Once again we see that our heavenly Father sets the same standards for those who would approach His throne; they have to come with humility and turn away from their sins. God promises that when those spiritual conditions are met, He will not only forgive sins but will also heal the land.

This shows that repentance is a major key to the healing we all need in our lives, as well as the healing that is needed in our land. If we will become that generation that will lay and establish a foundation for many generations, like Caleb, we will need to be repentant people. True repentance means making a complete turn. We have to turn completely from our worldly and fleshly ways and give ourselves to God fully. The great missionary to India E. Stanley Jones called the Church to full surrender. "You cannot cultivate an unsurrendered self. It is in the wrong center. You cannot discipline or cultivate a self which is off-center. The Center must be changed to Christ by surrender" (*Victory*, 113).

The idea here is that unless you surrender your life fully to the control of God's Spirit, you cannot be victorious in your Christian life.

Impact on other People

When you lay a foundation of full surrender and repentance, you will eventually realize that it is not only for or about you. Your life on earth affects other people around you. Any positive or negative act from anybody whether it is a spiritual or a physical act will produce fruit. No one is an island. Whatever you say or do affects and impacts other people around you. Being Kingdom minded means that I have to remember at all times that what I say, do or think has to be in accordance with God's will and purpose for my life and as established in His Word. The only way I can be certain of what is right and of edification to others is by, studying God's word, praying and seeking God's mind as well as being in fellowship with people of like precious faith.

> Being Kingdom minded means that I have to remember at all times that what I say, do or think has to be in accordance with God's will and purpose for my life and as established in His Word.

God's Grace

I should point out, however, that without God's enabling grace, none of us is capable of living the Christian life. When Paul was struggling with the thorn in his flesh, God's response to him was, "My grace is sufficient for you, for my strength is made perfect in weakness" (2 Corinthians 12:9). God's grace will always be sufficient for us whatever challenge, pain, or sorrow that comes our way. The scriptures promise that God will never allow you to face a temptation that is bigger than yourself. In Psalm 103:14, David affirms God's grace and mercy by stating that God knows our frame and remembers that we are just but dust. God knows you personally; there is nothing hidden in His sight. Actually, even the very thoughts you are about to think right now, he knows! (Psalms 139:2-4).

This knowledge should not lead us to shame, guilt or even fear but rather into His loving arms. His arms are ever open to receive us, as long as we come to Him in humility and contrite hearts.

Called to Intercede

When you become intimate with the Father, you will realize that you cannot just pray for yourself alone. You should not repent for your individual sins only; the Holy Spirit will always move you beyond your personal needs to the needs of the Kingdom. You can find this idea all over the scriptures. Abraham interceded for Sodom and Gomorrah, even though they were such a sinful people (Genesis 18:16-32). Moses interceded for the nation of Israel, especially when God was about to destroy the whole nation because of their stubbornness and unbelief (Numbers 14:13-19). Nehemiah interceded for the nation of Israel towards the end of the Babylonian captivity (Nehemiah 1:5-11). Daniel interceded for the nation, while in Babylon, and just like these other great men of God, he reminded God of His promises (Daniel 9:3-19).

> Therefore, we, too, have not repented and interceded enough until the pain and sorrow—the very burden of our families, our tribes, and our nations become our very own.

Therefore, we, too, have not repented and interceded enough until the pain and sorrow—the very burden of our families, our tribes, and our nations become our very own. I like the words that Nehemiah used to describe how he felt and how he bore the burden for his people when he got the report of the distress and reproach of the people of God in Judah. "So it was, when I heard these words that I sat down and wept, and mourned *for many* days; I was fasting and praying before the God of heaven". (Nehemiah 1:4).

191

We cannot do any less for our families and nations. We cannot just pray for ourselves. Any true man or woman of God should be concerned not only for their own families, but also for their communities and nations. This is what it means to be Kingdom minded. You cannot settle down and rejoice that you know the Lord without the burden for the needs of others and especially the lost-ness of the people who have not known Christ.

Books on Revival show us that the greatest revivals are born out of great prevailing, intercessory prayers. "… when you study revival long enough you inevitably find that there were people praying for revival when God poured out His Spirit upon the church" (Armstrong, 114). Throughout history God never sends revival or any great spiritual movements without this prerequisite of intercessory prayers from His people. Of late God has been laying the burden for intercessory prayer on many people's hearts. I personally feel we are on the verge of a great move of God.

Sin of Prayerlessness

When the nation of Israel requested Samuel the prophet to intercede for them, he said the following words. "Moreover, as for me, far be it for me that I should sin against the Lord in ceasing to pray for you; but I will teach you the good and the right way (1 Samuel 12:23).

According to Samuel the prophet, lack of intercessory prayers, especially in the life of a leader is sin! This is what is called a sin of "omission," as compared to the sin of "commission." If you are a child of God who lacks prayer in your life, you may not necessarily be involve in some great and atrocious sins, but still you will have sinned for lack of prayer. There is not one great man or woman of God that was not also a person of prayer. You will note that the greatest believers in history were not only men and women of prayer, but were especially involved in intercessory prayers.

Empty Religion

Going back to our chapter – Isaiah 58:2, we see yet another requirement or prerequisite for those men and women that the Lord would entrust with laying down foundations for future generations. When you first read the words of verse two, it seems as though the Lord is commending these people for their religious observances.

The Lord says, "Yet they seek me daily and delight to know my ways, as a nation that did righteousness and did not forsake the ordinances of their God. They ask of me the ordinances of justice. They take delight in approaching God" (Isaiah 58:2).

These people seem to have been doing the right religious things. Someone would ask, "Why religious people would be rebuked by the Lord, especially when they are involved in such religious activities?" Why would He reject their worship, and yet they are seeking Him daily?

> The hardest people to minister to are usually people who have been religious all their lives but have never had an encounter with God.

Apparently, these people had set up their own standards of worship as opposed or contrasted to God's standards. These people "sought" the Lord daily, and yet He rejected their worship. This is one passage that points to God's displeasure at empty religion.

Empty religion is worse than no religion at all! Personally I prefer or enjoy reaching out to people who are not religious at all more than people who have a form of godliness and yet have denied the power thereof (2 Timothy 3:5). The hardest people to minister to are usually people who have been religious all their lives but have never had an encounter with God. Many of these people have gone through all kinds of religious rituals and ceremonies. They have been baptized, confirmed, and have church membership cards, and yet they do not know Christ as

Lord of their lives.

Such people compare so well with the Israelites of Isaiah's day. God says that they performed their religious duties daily. They were as religious as could be, and yet did not honor the Lord in their lives. They lived for themselves, other than living for the Lord.

Just like the people in Malachi's day, these people could not understand why God could not acknowledge or endorse their spirituality (Isaiah 58:3, Malachi 2:14, 3:7). They actually asked the Lord as to why He did not recognize their religious act of fasting. "Why have we fasted, they say 'and you have not seen? Why have we afflicted our souls, and you take not notice?" (Isaiah 58:3). They were concerned that God had not recognized their religious acts, especially the act of fasting, which they considered to be a great sacrifice.

> God is sending a very clear message. He is never impressed by religious acts that lack the life of the Spirit in the, God have never been impressed by empty religion.

The Motive Matters

Our God is good and considerate. Even when we act foolishly and even ask rude and disrespectful questions, He still responds to us in love. This reminds me of David's words, "For He knows our frame; He remembers that we are dust" (Psalm 103:14). What a gracious and loving God we serve! He told these people that He was not necessarily opposed to their fasting. He was opposed to their attitudes and actions during their seasons of fasting. To God, it would be better that someone did not fast at all, rather than fasting with the wrong motive or attitude. The Lord took the time to explain to the Israelites what kind of fast or worship they should practice.

Oppression of Workers

First, the Lord rebukes them for how they dealt with their employees, even as they fasted. Fasting should never replace acts of mercy to those around us. We will need not only to be a praying and fasting community, but also be a people that treat those who work for us and our co-workers with respect. This is what will establish us as the generation that lays a strong foundation for many future generations. We will then impact both the present generation, but also positively impact numerous generations in the future.

The Lord tells His people, "You cannot hope to impress me by your fasting, while at the same time you do not care how you deal with those you relate with every day." God is sending a very clear message. He is never impressed by religious acts that lack the life of the Spirit in them. God has never been impressed by empty religion. Jesus did not come to make us religious. He came to give us new lives and also to make us new creations. "Therefore, if anyone is in Christ, he is a new creation; old things have passed away: behold, all things have become new" (2 Corinthians 4:17).

True Christianity is not a religion of special holy activities or rituals. True Christianity is a relationship with our loving heavenly Father. It is a lifestyle that is led and controlled by the Holy Spirit. Our brother Paul advises the Galatian believers, "Walk in the Spirit and you shall not fulfill the lust of the flesh" (Galatians 5:16). "You relate to God, respond to Him, and adjust your life so that He can do what He wants through you" (Blackaby, 39).

> It really does not matter who you are and how many titles you have or even how long you have been a believer. What matters most is for people to see your changed lifestyle and that you really care about others.

Our Lord told His disciples, "By this all will know that you are my disciples, if you have love for one another" (John 13:35). The idea here is; People will not be impressed by your religious acts, but will definitely be impacted by how much you care for those around you. It really does not matter who you are and how many titles you have or even how long you have been a believer. What matters most is for people to see your changed lifestyle and that you really care about others.

Sometime ago I met this person who really loved to talk about the Lord and the Bible at all times. However, talking to her did not feel like fellowship because she would always dominate whatever discussion people were having. She spoke so unceasingly and did not allow others in any group to talk. She acted a though she knew any subject better than everybody else! However, when things went wrong, she acted like a time bomb! She would respond in the most ungodly way I had ever seen. I could not believe the words that came out of her mouth. Her attitude during such times was even worse! One time after her constant tirades, I calmly responded to her, "I just wish that your love for the Lord and the Bible would be as intense as your words." She got my message and asked me to pray for her that she would cease from speaking too much and also to speak with consideration.

What I was telling this precious lady was the same message that God's prophet was telling the people in Isaiah chapter fifty-eight. The message was, "Let your words match your life; always remember that your conduct and lifestyle speak much louder than your words." This old saying is true, "Your actions are so loud that I cannot hear what you are saying."

Once I was doing a certain program with some colleagues. I noticed that their language was not what I had expected of Christian leaders. Some of the words they uttered were clearly not the kind expected of Christians, let alone Christian leaders. For quite some time I did not confront them about this behavior but finally I could not hold back. When I introduced the subject during one of our meetings, I could not believe the responses from some of these leaders. The most comical one was when two of the leaders said that this loose and careless talking was something they did only at the office but not at church or during membership gatherings! In other words for these Christian leaders it was alright and acceptable for them to use unacceptable language, as long as they were not in church or among their church members. What a double standard!

Importance of a Living Testimony

Talking of empty religion reminds me of a rather amusing event that took place in my life when I was thirteen or fourteen years old. This was about the time I came to know Christ as Lord. I had just spent a very tiring day working in my mother's garden. On my way home I stopped to relieve myself in woods since in the African country side we do not have as many public Restrooms. I left my work tool called a *"Jembe"* along the path. When I came back from the woods, the Jembe was gone! I looked everywhere because it was my mother's favorite Jembe. I was so frustrated and also afraid because I knew how much my mother loved this particular Jembe and now it was gone.

I went home with great trepidation and did not know how I could explain my carelessness to my mother. My mother was very understanding and even though she felt bad that I had lost her Jembe, she did not punish me for it. She only castigated me for leaving her Jembe along the path.

A few months later a neighbor lost her special leather rope, which, in those days was the best kind of rope for fetching firewood or for carrying water containers from the springs. A few days after this woman had lost her rope, she went from house to house asking the other women in Mbau-ini village whether they had seen her rope. One of the women by the name Julia responded, "Isn't that the rope that 'Mama so and so' gave to my mother when she visited me a while ago." It was quite a surprise because the lady who had given away this rope, which she had stolen, was not really a generous woman. That's why it was obvious to the other women that the lost rope was most likely the one she had given away. Most probably she gave it away when she realized that she might be found out.

The same villagers also found out that the same woman who had stolen the rope was the same woman who stole my mother's *Jembe*! Now the story makes a very strange twist! This very woman who was stealing people's *Jembes* and ropes also had a very sweet testimony of how the good Lord had saved her soul!

She was a staunch member our ***Tukutendereza*** fellowship.

Around this same time I came to know Christ as my Lord and Savior. I began doing personal Evangelism. I had great passion of wining people to Christ, and especially the people of my village and nearby villages and schools. One of the people I began witnessing to was my mother's friend Mama Michino who was one of our favorite neighbors. She had such a sweet spirit about her, and yet at that time she had not received Christ as Lord of her life. She was a most friendly, kind and generous lady. She had always treated me very kindly and therefore, I could not imagine her going to hell. I had to witness to her.

When I went to witness to Mama Michino about the love of Jesus, since she respected me a lot she would listen with great interest, but then when I asked her whether she would receive the Lord, she would often respond, "Hey, Kamau, before you get me saved, you will need to first of all get your Sister-in-the Lord, Mama so and so to return Mama Kamau's ***Jembe*** and Mama so and so's rope." Of course she would point out that her lifestyle was better off than that of this other ***Jembe***-stealing, rope-stealing Christian.

I found it very hard to present my case to Mama Michino because what she said was true. She was definitely a much better woman than the other woman and the whole village would have testified to that fact, and yet I knew that her good works would not win her a place in heaven. I kept praying for her and I thank the Lord that many years later I received the information that before this precious lady died she received Christ into her heart. I just hope that the other woman repented before she died.

Both of these women have now died, but that story remains fresh in my mind. We cannot laugh at this woman that was a thief because none of us can claim to have walked in the Spirit at all times. Even though we may not be stealing people's Jembes and ropes, there are definitely times or seasons when we have failed to walk in the Spirit.

When you realize that you are living in the flesh and that you are not practicing what you say, there is always a way out. Our

God is a forgiving God. He has not left us to die in our failures and sins. He has made a way of escape.

There is a verse in 1 John 2:1, which is rarely quoted by preachers because they feel that by quoting this verse they will have encouraged people to sin. The verse says, "My little children, these things I write to you, so that you may not sin. And if anyone sins, we have an advocate with the Father Jesus Christ the righteous. And He Himself is the propitiation for our sins, and not for ours only but also for the whole world"

John makes it clear that it is not God's will that we practice sin or that we intentionally go out and sin. If you are born of God, you will definitely know not to continue in sin (1 John 3:7-9). There is an illustration that I usually give when I preach on the subject of sin and forgiveness. I usually explain the nature of the pig as compared to the nature of the sheep. When a sheep falls into a muddy hole, it makes a lot of noise and struggles to get out of the mud. Not so for the pig! When a pig gets into a muddy hole, it begins to roll in the mud in sheer delight! Thank God he did not call us to be his precious pigs but his precious sheep! We are indeed the sheep of His pasture and the good shepherd knows our names and even when we walk through the roughest of valleys, His rod and staff will always comforts us (Psalm 23:4, 100:3, John 10:1-18).

I am sure this message is meant for someone who is reading this chapter right now. You may have gone through some experiences that made you think that the Lord would never forgive you. Listen to God's voice, "If we confess our sins, He is faithful and just to forgive us our sins and to cleanse us from all unrighteousness" (1 John 1:9). That's God's word for you today. Just repent and confess your sins to the Lord. He will forgive you of all your sins and restore you to Himself. You are God's sheep. You are not a pig! Just get out of the mire and allow the Lord to wash you by His precious blood.

Any Unforgivable Sins?

Discussing this subject remind me of a particular church in Kenya, which categorizes sins according to how deep some sins are. The leaders of this particular church teach that there are sins that are unforgivable. They usually expel from their membership any member who happens to fall into any of the "major sins," and yet retain other members who have the less serious sins.

I remember one time speaking to one of the senior leaders of this church. I pointed out to him the catalogue of sins found in Galatians 5:19-21. God says that those people who practice those things will not inherit the kingdom of God. I then pointed to some of the "less serious sins" in the list, as compared to the "major sins" that are categorized by this particular church. Some of the sins mentioned in this listing were not to be found in their list of "serious sins." For example: "selfish ambitions, dissensions, envy, hatred etc." However, those who continued practicing these sins will not inherit the kingdom of God, even though their sins may seem inconsequential.

I agreed with this preacher that some sins have greater and much more painful consequences than others. For example, someone who commits fornication or adultery and in the process gets someone pregnant or contacts a contagious disease will definitely experience greater pain, regret, and even greater consequences than someone who lusted but did not go out and fulfill his lustful desires by being involved in prostitution, fornication, or adultery. The consequences of sin differ, but God considers all sin to be wrong and abhorrent to his holiness. However, we need to know that all sins are forgivable. I think that the only sin that is unforgivable is unbelief. If you refuse to acknowledge the love of God and the love of Jesus on the cross of Calvary, then definitely your unbelief will lead you straight to hell. Jesus made it clear that there is no other way to the Father. He is the way, the truth and the life (John 14:6).

> The consequences of sin differ, but God considers all sin to be wrong and abhorrent to his holiness.

Our joy and confidence is not necessarily because we have never sinned, since we came to know Christ as our Savior and Lord, because most likely each of us has sinned. Of course I would rejoice with anyone who has never sinned since he or she came to Christ. However our joy is that we have faith in a loving heavenly Father who has made a way of escape for us. "The blood of Jesus, God's own son cleanses us from all sins (1 John 1:7). Thank God for the blood of the Lamb of God. I love that old hymn that speaks of the fountain of blood drawn from Immanuel's veins. One of the verses says, "Dear dying lamb, Thy precious blood shall never lose it power. Till all the ransomed church of God be saved to sin no more." Praise the Lord that the blood shall never lose its power.

Most times we quote these verses about the power of the blood of Christ when witnessing to people who do not know Christ. Even if that is alright, we often forget that John was not writing to the unbelievers. The Epistles of first, second and third John were addressed to the believers. It is the believers that needed to confess their sins and receive the cleansing power of the blood of Jesus.

I pray that every one of you reading this book has already received this forgiveness of sin. If you have not received Christ, then you will need to confess your sins to Him. The scripture says, "If you confess with your mouth the Lord Jesus, and believer in your heart that God has raised Him from the dead, you will be saved" (Romans 10:9). It's as easy as that. If you do not know Christ as Lord, please allow me to lead you to Him. Please say this prayer and mean it from your heart: "Dear Lord Jesus, I come to you. I acknowledge and appreciate the fact that you loved me and came to earth to save me. I repent of my sin and ask you to forgive me and cleanse me by your own blood. I invite you into my heart. Come and be my Lord and Savior. I believe that you've come into me according to your promise. Thank you for saving me. Fill me with your power that I might live for you all the days of my life. I ask this in your precious Name. Amen.

After you have prayed this prayer, you will then need to share your story with someone else. Please do not keep this to yourself. Tell someone else of your new-found faith in Christ, and also seek for a good church in which to fellowship, and thus grow in your spiritual life.

Armstrong Cheggeh

Lessons From Chapter 11

IF WE WILL BECOME that generation that establishes a foundation for many generations, like Caleb, we will need to be repentant people. True repentance means making a complete turn. We have to turn completely from our worldly and fleshly ways and give ourselves to God fully.

The only way I can be certain of what is right and of edification to others is by, studying God's word, praying and seeking God's mind as well as being in fellowship with people of like precious faith.

When you become intimate with the Father, you will realize that you cannot just pray for yourself alone. Actually, you cannot repent for your individual sins only. The Holy Spirit will always move you beyond your personal needs to the needs of the Kingdom.

We have not repented and interceded enough until the pain and sorrow—the very burden of our families, our tribes, and our nations become our very own.

Throughout history God never sends revival or any great spiritual movements without this prerequisite of intercessory prayers from His people.

According to Samuel the prophet, lack of intercessory prayers, especially in the life of a leader is sin! This is more what is called a sin of "omission," as compared to the sin of "commission." If you are a child of God who lacks prayer in your life, you may not necessarily be involve in some great and atrocious sins, but still you will have sinned for lack of prayer.

Our God is good and considerate. Even when we act foolishly and even ask rude and disrespectful questions, He still responds to us in love.

God is never impressed by religious acts that lack the life of the Spirit in them. He has never been impressed by empty religion. *Jesus did not come to make us religious. He came to give us new lives and also to make us new creations.*

True Christianity is not a religion of special holy activities or rituals. True Christianity is a relationship with our loving heavenly Father. It is a lifestyle that is led and controlled by the Holy Spirit.

People will not be impressed by your religious acts, but will definitely be impacted by how much you care for those around you. It really does not matter who you are and how many titles you have or even how long you have been a believer. What matters most is for people to see your changed lifestyle and that you really care about each other.

Let your words match your life. Always remember that your conduct and lifestyle speak much louder than your words.

Our joy and confidence is not necessarily because we have never sinned, since we came to know Christ as our Savior and Lord, because most likely each of us has sinned. Our joy is that we have faith in a loving heavenly Father who has made a way of escape for us, as we repent of our sins and yield to His will and purpose in our lives.

Conclusion: What I Leave Behind Matters

THE CONTENTS OF THIS BOOK remind us that whatever we think, say, or do will not leave us in a neutral ground. Our lives affect and impact others negatively or positively every single day of our lives. For this reason, every child of God needs to live with eternity in their minds. We leave behind landmarks and legacies wherever we go, whether we know it or not and whether we like it or not. You leave legacies and impacts every day of your life.

Life will definitely have challenges, and like Caleb we will need to constantly stand strong even in times of trials and afflictions, realizing that God's grace and power will always be available to those who choose to pursue Him whatever the cost. Our courage and boldness will be enhanced by the fact that God's promises are firm and changeless. God can be trusted to take care of His own (See Hebrews 13:5b, Deuteronomy 31:6).

Every one of us needs to be reminded to trust in the Lord in the darkest of hours. Our brother Caleb was elevated to very high levels of spiritual leadership not by the praise of men, but more by the challenges and oppositions he experienced. Through this story and many other stories in the Bible and church history, we come to realize that there are times that the Lord will allow trials to come into our lives; not to destroy us, but more to elevate us and also to bring greater glory to His great Name.

God's word is the standard that helps us know how to respond in times of challenge, as well as in our everyday lives. What the Lord responds to when we pray is not our wishful thinking, but rather utterances that are based on His written word. A prayer that is prayed in accordance to God's will as established in His word will always receive God's response.

One of the greatest hindrances to flowing in the power and the anointing of God is the spirit of fear. The Bible tells us that God has not given us the spirit of fear, but of power, love and a sound mind (2 Timothy 1:7). When faced by fearful situations, we need to always be reminded of God's care and love for His children. We also need to know that the only time the Lord will allow situations of fear or suffering in our lives is when the experience will leave us in a better place spiritually or bring greater glory to Him. The best place to be is in His will, plan, and purpose.

God allowed most of His generals in the Bible as well as in the history of the church to go through trials and sometimes great afflictions, as part of their ministry preparations. It seems that the wilderness school is an imperative to God's generals.

From the story of Caleb, we come to understand that sometimes the Lord will call His servants to stand alone, and that sometimes the truth is in the hands of the minority.

God will sometimes call the minority to stand for him against all odds. Sometimes He will remove the pain or the challenge like He did in the case of Joshua and Caleb, but at times He may allow the believers to suffer; not because He is sadistic, but because He knows the end from the beginning (Isaiah 46:10). God will only allow those things that will build us up spiritually; cause us to be kingdom minded, and bring greater glory to Him. Some of those things might at times include suffering for Him.

Our faith in God should be the foundation upon which all other activities are established. Our faith should be lived out in a way that affects the people around us in a positive way. Our homes and families should be the place where our lives of leaving behind a righteous legacy are established, as we raise our children in a godly environment.

Every decision we make impacts not only our individual lives, but the lives of numerous people that we encounter every day, and especially our own families. Our prayer then should not only be that we live long lives, but rather that every day we will impact those that we encounter with and thus leave a righteous legacy.

One of the greatest gifts the Lord blesses us with is the gift of solid friendships. Good friends are a great asset both in family life, as well as in the ministry. God Himself wants to be friends with His children. He is the friend that sticks closer than a brother (Proverbs 18:24b).

Good friendships and lasting relationships call for commitment and sacrifice. All good friendships call for reciprocity. Each friend has to invest in the friendship. The Bible says, "A man *who has* friends must himself be friendly" (Proverbs 18:24a). Such friendships become very useful, especially in times of challenge. Therefore, we should be very careful of the people we allow into our lives.

Forgiveness is one of the most significant aspects of a lasting friendship; it is accepting the fact that even the best of friends can make mistakes. We should always be ready to forgive, and reject the spirit of un-forgiveness, if we are to experience the blessing and joy of a lasting friendship.

Our friendship and intimacy with God will definitely be the most important relationship and will also affect what we become and what kind relationships we have with each other, and also the quality of service we render to our heavenly Father. When we know Him well, we will not wait for a better season to serve Him; we will serve Him at all times even in the wilderness of life. He makes it possible to praise Him in the wilderness experiences.

When we gain an intimacy with the Father and as we grow in His word, we will understand that there is no problem bigger than God's promise. He obligates Himself to fulfil His word as long as we meet the conditions on which those promises are established.

God knows our desires and dreams, and is willing and able to meet every need, as long as the request is in accordance to His word. Since we are children of His love, there is no request that is too good, or too great for us.

Every believer needs to understand that the Kingdom of God revolves around God's will and purpose. However, sincere our prayers are, even when they include fasting will not move God's hand unless they are prayed in accordance to His will and purpose for us as established in His word.

As parents, we will need to lead by example. Our children are our first and most important church. Before we emphasize our local church ministries and activities, we should emphasize the Family altar. One of the most important aspects of a godly parent is the words they speak. What we say to each other as couples and what we tell our children matter a lot; it affects the future of our children. If we speak words of love, faith, and support to our children, we will most likely raise a godly heritage. The children will grow to be loving and caring adults.

> Every believer needs to understand that the Kingdom of God revolves around God's will and purpose..

Responsible parents will not hold back from disciplining their children. All discipline should be done with a heart of love and concern. Discipline should never be destructive to the children; it should be applied firmly with love and fairness.

Children should not only be disciplined when they are wrong, but should be praised and encouraged when they do good. The idea should be to invest so well in the children that their generation becomes better than parent's generation.

Even with the prayer and the study of God's word, every child of God needs to understand that none of us can gain a full and perfect knowledge of God and His will and purpose for us. Any of us can fail and not walk in God's will at times. That's why it is important to understand and appreciate God's forgiveness. As long as we are willing to acknowledge our shortcomings and sin; and as long as we are willing to confess our sin, God promises to forgive our sins and cleanse us from all our unrighteousness (1 John 1:7-9).

There is great power for the believers who practice prayer and fasting in their lives. The believers who practice prayer and fasting have great power of defeating demonic powers. We find that both in the Bible as well as in church history, all of God's generals were men and women who practiced prayer and fasting. However, prayer and fasting should always be accompanied by sincerity and purity of life, for it to produce results.

God calls us to be a church that touches the world with His love and grace. We should try our best to present Christ to those around us by ministering to the physical, social and spiritual needs of those around us.

Repentance is such a big word to any true believer. Our spiritual foundations will be much better if and when we practice repentance. This repentance should include intercessory prayers where we pray for our families, tribes, and nations. We have to live lives of total surrender to the Lord if we are to establish the foundations for many future generations.

Lives of repentance and intercessory prayers are the, "seed beds," for revival. There is not one revival that ever took place without a season of prayer and fasting from some groups of believers.

True Christianity is therefore, not a religion of special holy activities or rituals, but rather a relationship with the Lord; a life controlled by God's Spirit. Such a life will give us joy and confidence as we continue serving the Lord. We will indeed become that generation that establishes foundations for many future generations.

Armstrong Cheggeh

Bibliography

Allen, Ronald B. (Gen. Editor: Gaebelein, Frank E.), <u>The Expositor's Bible Commentary, Vol. 2</u>, Grand Rapids: Zondervan Publishing House, 1990.

Armstrong, John H. <u>True Revival: What happens when God's Spirit moves</u>, Eugene, OR: Harvest House Publishers, 2001.

Arnold, Clinton. (General Editor) <u>Zondervan Exegetical Commentary on the New Testament,</u>, Grand Rapids, MI: Zondervan Publishing House, 2010.

Atwood, Will. <u>Here and Coming…as it is in heaven</u>, Carrolton, TX: Ekklesia Society Publications, 2007.

Blackaby, Henry and King, Claude V. <u>Experiencing God</u>, Nashville, TN: Broadman and Holman Publishers, 1998.

Blackaby, Henry and Blackaby Richard. <u>Spiritual Leadership</u>, Nashville, TN: B & H. Publishing Group, 2011.

Bonem, Mike and Patterson, Roger. <u>Leading from the Second Chair</u>, San Francisco: Jossey Bass, 2005.

Briggs, Kenneth. <u>The Power of Forgiveness</u>, Minneapolis, MN: Fortress Press, 2008.

Brown, Lesley (Editor), "Legacy," <u>The Shorter Oxford English Dictionary on Historical Principles</u>, VOL. 1, Oxford: Clarendon Press, 1993.

Carmichael, Amy. <u>This One Thing</u>, London: Oliphants Ltd., 1950.

Carre, Captain E. G. <u>Praying Hyde: A challenge to Prayer</u>, London: Pickering & Inglis, 1950.

Cheggeh, Armstrong. <u>Developing Relationships with Integrity</u>,

Lake Mary, FL: Creation House Publishers, 2010.

Crisp, Oliver and Sweeney, Douglas A. <u>After Jonathan Edwards: The course of the New England Theology</u>, New York: Oxford University Press, 2012.

Cuthbert, Nick. <u>How to survive and thrive as a church Leader</u>, Oxford: Monarch Books, 2006.

Dodds, Elisabeth D. Marriage to a Difficult Man: The Uncommon Union of Jonathan and Sara Edwards, Philadelphia: The Westminster Press, 1971.

Duewel, Wesley L. <u>Ablaze for God,</u> Grand Rapids: Francis Asbury Press, 1989.

Eisenman, Tom L. The Accountable Man, pursuing integrity through trust and friendship, Downers Grove, IL: InterVasity press, 2004.

Faust, Clarence H. and Johnson, Thomas H. Jonathan Edwards: Representative selections, with introduction, bibliography and Notes, New York: Hill and Wang, 1967.

Franklin, Jentezen. Fasting: Opening the door to a deeper, more intimate, more powerful relationship with God, Lake Mary, Charisma House, 2008.

Ford, Stephanie. <u>Kindred souls; Connecting thorough spiritual friendship</u>, Nashville, TN: Upper room books, 2006.

Garner, Eric. "Team Building: The most Rewarding Act of Leadership," http://www.zeromillion.com/business/teambuilding.html#ixzz0YUveJ1O7

Gitau, Boniface G. <u>Making Wise Choices in Life: Wisdom for Every Day Living</u>, 2nd Revised Edition, Cincinnati, OH: Vessel of Honor International Ministries, 2012.

Hagee, John. <u>Day of Deception</u>, Nashville, TN: Thomas Nelson Publishers, 1997.

Hanson, Paul D. Interpretation: A Bible commentary for Teaching and Preaching, Isaiah 40–66, Louisville, KY: John Knox Press, 1995.

Henry, Mathew. "2 Kings 4:1-7" Matthew Henry's Commentary on the whole Bible, Volume 2, Peabody, MA: Hendrickson Publishers, 1998, pp. 563-564.

Hill, Andrew and Walton, John H. A survey of the Old Testament, Grand Rapids: Zondervan Publishing House, 1991.

Jones, E. Stanley. Victory Through Surrender, Nashville, TN: Abingdon Press, 1966.

Kimnach, Wilson H. Minkema, Kenneth P. and Sweeney, Douglas A. "A Farewell Sermon preached at the First Precinct in Northampton, After the People's Public Rejection of Their Minister... on June 22, 1750," The Sermons of Jonathan Edwards, A Reader, New Haven: Yale University Press, 1999, pp. 212-241.

Lamb, Jonathan. Integrity leading with God watching, Nottingham, England: Intervasity Press, 2006.

Lindsay, Hal. Combat Faith, New York, Bantam Books, 1986.

Lloyd-Jones, D. Martyn. Faith, Tried and Triumphant, Grand Rapids: Baker Book House, 1992.

McCullum, Hugh. Africa's Broken Heart: The land the World Forgot, Geneva: WCC Publication, 2006.

Miller, Calvin. Into the Depths of God, Minneapolis, MN: Bethany House Publishers, 2000.

Miller, C. John. Repentance: A daring call to real surrender, Fort Washington, PA: CLC publication, 2009.

Munroe, Myles. Becoming a Leader, Lanham, MD: Pneuma Life Publishing, 1993.

Munroe, Myles. Passing it On, New York: Faith word Hachette book Group, 2011.

Nkurumah, Kwame. I speak of Freedom: A statement of African Ideology, New York: Frederick A. Praeger, 1962.

Njuguna, Geoffrey Kamau. Becoming a Secure Leader: The Perils of an Insecure Leader, n.p, Nairobi, 2015.

Nzeketha, Joseph Mukuna. Is there Hope for the Church: Redirecting the Millennial Church back to the Original Mission, n.p, Xulon Press, 2013.

Packer, J. I. Rediscovering Holiness, Ann Arbor, MI: Servant Publications, 1992.

Piper, John. And Taylor, Justin. A God Entranced Vision of All Things: The Legacy of Jonathan Edwards, Wheaton, Crossway Books, 2004.

Quinsey et al. Juvenile Delinquency: Understanding the Origins of Individual Differences, Washington DC: American Psychological Association, 2004.

Rand, Ron. For Fathers who aren't in Heaven, Ventura, CA: Regal Books, 1986.

Shackelford, Don. et al. Truth for Today Commentary: An Exegesis & Application of the Holy Scriptures, Search, AR: Resource Publications, 2005.

Smith, William. Smith's Bible Dictionary, Peabody, MA: Hendrickson Publishers, 1999.

Stott, John. Basic Christian Leadership, Biblical Models of Church, Gospel and ministers, Downers Grove, IL: InterVarsity Press, 2002.

Strong, James. "Greek Dictionary of the New Testament," The Exhaustive Concordance of the Bible, Mclean, VA: Macdonald Publishing Company, 1990, p. 59.

Strong, James. "Greek Dictionary of the New Testament" The New Strong's Expanded Exhaustive Concordance of the Bible, Dallas: Thomas Nelson Publishers, 2010, p. 43. 92.

Townsend, John. Leadership Beyond Reason, Nashville, TN: Thomas Nelson, 2009.

Vaughan, David. A divine light: The spiritual leadership of Jonathan Edwards, Nashville, TN: Cumberland House Publishing, 2007.

Wesley, John. The Sum of all True Religion, Nicholasville, KY: Schmul Publishing Company, 2014.

Wigglesworth, Smith. Smith Wigglesworth On Faith, New Kensington, PA: Whitaker House, 1998.

Wiersbe, Warren. On Being a Leader for God, Grand Rapids, MI: Baker books, 2011.

Winslow, Ola Elizabeth. Jonathan Edwards 1703-1758, New York: Collier Books, 1961.

Zahnd, Brian. Unconditional? The call of Jesus to Radical forgiveness, Lake Mary, FL: Charisma house, 2010.

Armstrong Cheggeh

About the Author

DR. ARMSTRONG KAMAU CHEGGEH has been involved in numerous ministries over the last forty-three years. He began preaching at the age of sixteen in 1972, while in High School.

Dr. Cheggeh is the Presiding Bishop and General Overseer of the Fountain of Life Churches, International, including those in Kenya, Uganda, Tanzania, Rwanda, Burundi, D.R. Congo, Zambia and India. Dr. Cheggeh conducts Marriage Enrichment Seminars across the USA and Africa. He is a sought-after speaker in Marriage enrichment seminars, and church leadership conferences.

Through his powerful and, dynamic ministry, Dr. Cheggeh has impacted thousands of people in the continents of Africa, Asia, Europe, and North America. Dr. Cheggeh has a rich Apostolic anointing that touches the nations for Christ. He is a graduate of Rosedale Bible College in Irwin, Ohio, with a double major Diploma in Christian Education and Pastoral Ministries. Dr. Cheggeh continued his education at Central Bible College with a BA in Bible and Vanguard University of Southern California where he received an MA in Religion.

After his return to Africa he studied at Nairobi International School of Theology and received an MA in Christian Ministries. He later returned to the USA and studied and graduated from Asbury Theological Seminary with a Doctor of Ministry Degree (D.Min) in leadership and preaching. Dr. Cheggeh and his wife of 35 years have five grown children and three grandchildren.

Armstrong Cheggeh

Contact the Author

drcheggeh@gmail.com
http://folcinternational.com

Made in the USA
Lexington, KY
30 March 2017